MAKING WAY: A MEMOIR

Mitch Taylor

© 2021 Mitch Taylor

All rights reserved. No part of this book may be reproduced by any means without the prior permission of the author, with the exception of brief passages in reviews.

Taylor, Mitch, 1944-, author
Making Way: A Memoir / Mitch Taylor.

ISBN: 978-1-7776798-0-4 (paper)

1. Taylor, Mitchell Joseph. 2. Memoirs (form). 3. Business enterprises - Canada - Vancouver - History - 20th century.

Editor Jillian Lerner
Design Stacey Noyes, LuzForm Design
Typeset in Whitman

*To Ian, Taya, Sophie, and Matias,
I love you forever.*

CONTENTS

INTRODUCTION   1

1. SETTING OUT ON MY OWN   7
   | *Impish Ways: Hypnotized Chickens and Other Shocks*   26
   | *A Sincere Apology*   34
   | *A Calf Scramble Explained*   39

2. ODD JOBS   43

3. THE OPEN ROAD & THE CORPORATE LADDER   61
   | *Why I Don't Play Poker*   86

4. CREEKHOUSE INDUSTRIES & GRANVILLE ISLAND   97

5. FALSE CREEK MARINAS   113
   | *A Fire, A Rabbit, and a Naked Lady*   128
   | *Maurice Tackles a Dasher*   130
   | *Harold's Maiden Voyage*   132
   | *The Stakeout*   136
   | *Jeans*   146

6. THE OWL, THE ENGINEER & THE GOLDEN MOVEMENT EMPORIUM AUCTION   151
   | *Cable Television to the Caribbean*   164

7. GRANVILLE ISLAND BREWING   173
   | *Negotiations with a Telephone Company*   194
   | *Mister Goold Works for Free*   198
   | *We've Got Your Back Mitch*   201
   | *A Nightmare in DC*   204
   | *Mon Ami à la Vie*   208

8. IT'S ONLY A FLESH WOUND   215
   | *Inspector Clouseau Visits Sarlat-la-Canéda*   230

9. WORDS OF ADVICE   239

10. BELLINGHAM MARINE   257
    | *An Illegal Apple*   292

11. SEA FEVER   297
    | *Antiguan Customs & Immigration Explained*   330

12. NOT THE RETIRING TYPE   337

    CONCLUSION   355

    ACKNOWLEDGEMENTS   379

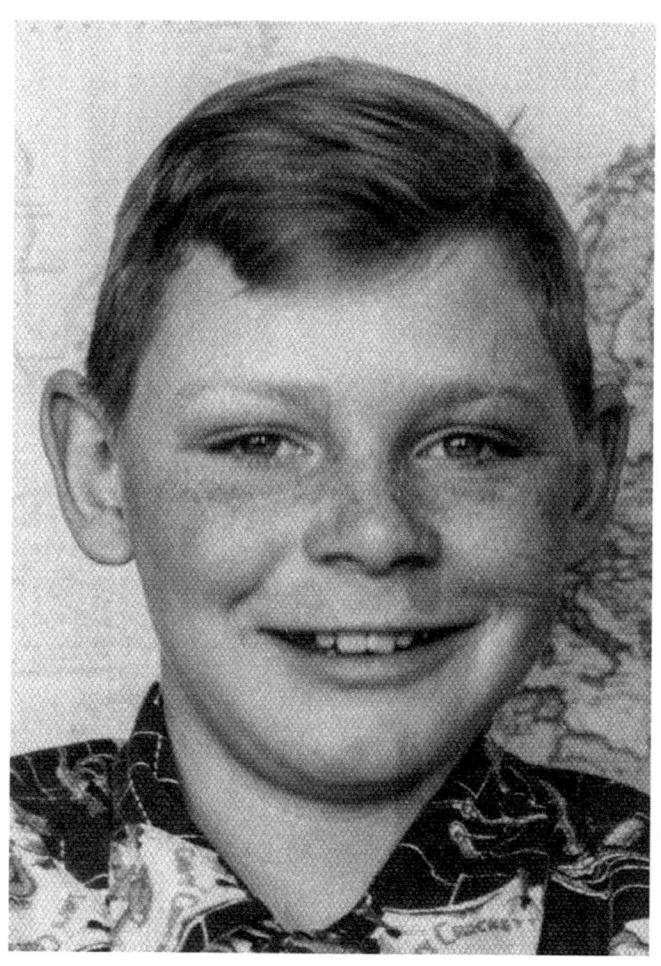

School picture, Mitch, age 10.

INTRODUCTION

I've lived a life that's full
I travelled each and every highway
And more. Much more than this, I did it
   my way

Paul Anka, "My Way"

Over the next pages I invite you to consider the implausible journey of a young boy who grew up in the 1950s in a poor farming community in Manitoba. Because he was smart and he was much loved and supported, he came away from that farm feeling that he could do and become just about anything he wanted. You can look on as he gets an education, works at dreadful and exciting jobs, travels, and opens his mind and prospects to a vast world in waiting. The farm boy becomes a man and though his cheekiness never fades, he eventually matures into a worthy husband, father, friend, decision-maker, and advice-giver.

He also evolves into a creative entrepreneur, with a keen sense of future opportunities and an ability to imagine what others ignored, such as the promising wasteland of Vancouver's False Creek in the late 1960s. By then he possessed enough skills and chutzpah to develop prosperous enterprises that have since changed the face and fabric of the city.

I know this all sounds pretty grand and a bit over the top, but I do have to entice you to get totally involved in this tale and then you can decide for yourself. After all, I am still a salesman at 76 years old.

Along the way there are some astounding scenes and a lot of ups and downs, just like a game of snakes and ladders. We will sit confidently at the Imperial Oil boardroom table in Toronto with a 27 year old analyst emboldened by his position in the President's office. We will raise an inaugural glass of Granville Island Lager from the first craft brewery in Canada. We will cower fearfully in a tent in the wild Cariboo while a drunken fool tries to force us into a game of Russian roulette. There will be tears as the wheels come off the family bus, and no end of giggles as a stark naked Mitchie, stranded in the hallway of the Hay-Adams Hotel in Washington DC, looks imploring into the eyes of Abe Lincoln.

Read on dear friend, it's the best that irrepressible young man can do for you.

What follows is a collection of stories about how I made my way in the world, along with glimpses of how the world has changed from 1944 to 2020. There will be prodigious challenges, lessons learned, and self-awareness gradually acquired in this recounting of pivotal experiences. But I won't give it all away just yet. In many ways it is a classic narrative: an ordinary human's journey of discovery, self-discovery, and growing recognition of the relationships that make it possible.

INTRODUCTION

At the outset I should set some expectations for my readers, and perhaps dampen others. This is a personal memoir, with an emphasis on my adventures in entrepreneurship, interspersed with some of the colourful anecdotes and eccentric personalities that made life interesting along the way. It is not at all a comprehensive account of all our important life events and treasured relationships with family and close friends, nor does it do justice to all the wonderful people I care about and am most grateful for. I humbly apologize to any of my cherished relatives, buddies, and associates who might find themselves left out or insufficiently mentioned in these pages. A complete account of all the people I carry in my heart would be a different and much more extensive project.

In this wee book I have gathered only a few of the memorable snapshots I've held on to as the years flew by. The genesis of this collection was our long dining room table at Marpole Avenue and the rousing tales of derring-do that got shared there as I occasionally recounted for our family and friends some of the more compelling moments of my youth and early business ventures. Virtually every time I indulged in these memories someone would say, "Mitch that is an incredible story! You really must write a book one day before you forget all the details. Your grandchildren will surely thank you."

So that dear reader, is what you have in your hands. This book is dedicated to my much-loved grandchildren Matias, Sophie, Taya, and Ian.

A memoir is by definition a work of non-fiction. I hereby certify that everything I have written here is true, to the very best of my knowledge. If a reader finds that some date or account of events does not coincide with their own recollection, I apologize. This is my recollection of experiences that transpired some many years ago and I accept the possibility that my brain is not quite as "Mitchell Sharp" (with credit to Gillian Woolliams for the nickname) as it once was.

Sit down, relax, pour yourself a cup of tea or pint of beer and enjoy the tale.

Mitch Taylor
Vancouver, January 2021

First picture of Mitch after settling in with the Browns in 1952, age 8.

— 1 —

SETTING OUT ON MY OWN

When I was seven years old, I boarded a train that would propel me 400 miles from home. The journey would take about ten hours. I didn't realize it at the time, but I would never return to live with my parents. Racing west through the countryside, I was suspended between two humble outposts that had very little in common: Fort Frances, Ontario is timber country surrounded by lakes and forests, while Regent, Manitoba stretches out in patchwork farms and flat prairies. Their main connection is proximity to the two iconic Canadian railways and their ubiquitous lines of red brick railway stations, sidings, and section houses at every stop. Only Fort Frances rates notice in the *National Geographic Atlas of the World*.

I was on my way to live with a couple I had never met. Alexander and Winnifred Brown farmed a half section of land three miles west of Regent in the southwest corner of Manitoba. My brother Bob, five years my senior, had spent the previous school year boarding with the Browns and working on their farm. He had great stories of the place, but he had been lonely and encouraged me to join him for the next school year. I was irrepressibly eager at the prospect, and with my parents' permission, the two of us set out in August of 1952 to get settled at the Browns before the start of classes in September.

Although I was about to turn eight, I had never attended school. There was no local school where I grew up, just like there was no local hospital, library, bank, nor any shops. My family lived thirty miles east of Fort Frances at a tiny remote stop on the Canadian National rail line called Farrington, where they carved out a subsistence, living with no neighbours in the all-but-abandoned railway hamlet. We ate what we could grow, forage, hunt and fish for, along with stores of flour, canned goods, and dehydrated peas.

My parents had learned about the Browns from an advertisement in the newspaper. Alex Brown was the secretary treasurer of the Coxworth School Board. The grandness of that title dims slightly when you find out that the school board had only one school and that school had only seven students. The one-room country schoolhouse was located near the Hathaway railway siding, which also boasted the Hathaway Pool Elevator, a one-sheet curling rink and the elevator operator's house. The school needed at least eight students to receive a provincial grant to continue operating. The previous year the Browns, who had no children of their own, had placed an ad in the *Winnipeg Free Press* seeking a boy who could come to live with them, help on their farm, and attend the local school. Since the only schooling available in Farrington was through correspondence courses, my parents were happy to seize this chance to get their children a better education. Bob made the trial run in 1951, and then the two of us sallied forth together in 1952.

The fall harvest was in full swing as the train clickety-clacked across the flat, endless prairies and whistled shrilly as we approached every level crossing. In some fields the crops stood waiting, their heads bent with the weight of mature grains. Other sections had already been swathed, leaving one long continuous windrow of neatly cut stalks winding around and around the field from the outside to the center. Combine harvesters laboriously chewed up the dried stalks and spewed out dusty clouds of scattered straw. Trucks and grain wagons waited to unload the golden grain and transfer it to round metal granaries clustered near the farm buildings. To a young boy every vista was new and tremendously exciting. I'm sure I asked Bob countless questions and learned as much as I could about tractor-pulled and self-propelled combine harvesters, and how to recognize the different types of vehicles and farm equipment. I was about to become a lifelong aficionado of Massey Harris combines, Ford trucks, and Minneapolis Moline tractors. I was totally enchanted with the many shades of golden crops, the picture-perfect farmyards with their orderly rows of shining granaries, and the endless fields that stretched on and on as far as the eye could see.

On the journey I suppose I had ample time to consider what this next stage of life was going to be like for me. It's not easy to fathom what one's seven-year old self might have been feeling. I must have been more than a little apprehensive facing so many uncertainties: would I miss my parents, would the Browns like me, would I sink or swim at school? But honestly what I remember most is being thrilled about this adventure and very keen to go to a real school. It may sound like revisionist history to say this now, but I recall arriving at a major decision in that slow moving railway carriage, as I woke up somewhere west of Winnipeg. I had ample reason to be forlorn and anxious if I focused on leaving home and looking backward. Almost everything before me was unknown. But I chose to look forward, to be optimistic and enthusiastic about the challenges and opportunities ahead of me. I was embarking on an entirely new life with the Browns and I was determined to take full advantage of every part of that experience. I would learn to read and write. I would eat well, work hard, and lighten some of the burden on my folks. I would learn how the world worked. I would fully embrace this new life that was about to unfold at the next station.

I did not have to worry about the Browns who welcomed us warmly at the Brandon North railway siding. They were kind and soft-spoken folks in their fifties. Alex, in his fedora and Sunday suit, had a lean and deeply suntanned face and soft dark eyes that crinkled when he smiled. Winnifred—in her librarian glasses and best dress, her hair in a bun—wore a broad welcoming smile and spread her arms to embrace me before we ever exchanged a word. Soon we were happily driving south down Highway 10 towards Boissevain in their old 1929 Marquette to my new home in Regent. The Marquette's twenty-three year old transmission had a bad habit of popping out of third gear every time Mister Brown took his foot off the gas. My first "big important job" in the Brown family was to sit beside him in the front middle seat and hold the floor mounted gear shifter firmly in third until he needed to downshift.

We had to agree on practical names and since I already had a mom and dad and we were only boarding with the Browns we agreed on Uncle Alex and Aunt Winnifred, soon shortened to Uncle and Auntie. When describing her in the third person we adopted the much more reverent, "The Aunt," as the proper title for the matriarch of the family. Most of our friends followed suit. I called Uncle "Unc" and he began fondly referring to me as "the boy."

I had a lot of catching up to do. I was eight that September 7th of 1952 and should have been going into grade two, but I had not learned to read or write yet. It was decided that I would take grade one and two together that next year. Auntie was confident that we were both up for this challenge; she had been a schoolteacher up until a few years prior, and she knew a clever boy when she saw one. At least she knew how to nurture and motivate one. She had a special talent for inspiring confidence, and I could feel that she believed in me. All that school year we both worked very hard to teach little Mitchie how to read properly. By June of 1953 I had caught up and would be ready to start grade three with the other kids my age.

The first few months were a bit rough. I had a lisp that needed correction. My F's and S's were equal in sound and many a dirty look followed my improper descriptions. Any teasing at school was short-lived. I gave one of the perpetrators a bloody nose and his attitude improved quickly, as did my diction under The Aunt's tutelage. I also had weak legs and couldn't run very far or fast. That was the lingering result of a bout with polio my mother and I suffered together in 1950. I don't remember much of that illness beyond a dreary hot summer spent lying immobile on a mattress that had been dragged outside onto the open porch so we could watch the clouds float by. That physical diminishment was soon fixed by lots of exercise on the farm, where every day included endless walking, running, cycling, and exploring.

Daily life on the Brown farm was typical of most households in the area. We cultivated grain and raised cattle, egg-laying hens, chickens, pigs, and a couple hundred baby chickens and turkeys each spring. We milked the cows at 530 in the morning and again at 530 at night, yes twice a day. Never ever could you miss a milking for the milk would dry up. We drew off the rich fat from the milk in a hand cranked "cream separator" and sold the big cans of cream to the Souris Creamery, whose truck called around every few days. We didn't sell our milk. Milk for human consumption came from more industrialized dairy farms with large capital investments in specialized equipment and dairy cows that produced much more milk than our little herd. Our cows were bred to produce calves destined eventually for the dinner table; milk was a secondary product. We drank what we wanted and fed the leftover milk to the animals. Selling the cream and the eggs produced the only steady cash generated by the farm, a meagre income augmented by the monthly government child allowance cheque, the sale of grain and dressed turkeys in the fall and the sale of fattened steers in the spring. We were not very well off but, of course, I did not know that nor thank goodness did I care. We always ate well and had warm clothes (I would get two new pairs of lined jeans in the winter and two new pairs of regular jeans in the spring) and we enjoyed many good times with friends and each other. It was a very happy idyllic farm boyhood. Young readers might be interested to know this was possible without the internet or computers. We had electricity and a telephone but no indoor flush toilets, clothes drier or dishwasher.

My brother Bob decided to return home to our parents after a few years but I chose to stay with the Browns permanently. I suspect the transition was more difficult for Bob as he was a teenager, already itching to leave school and start working. After the first year I had settled into a happy long-term "keeper" relationship with Auntie and Uncle. We had formed a lasting bond and none of us could imagine dissolving it. That relationship formed the essential building blocks of what would become my lifelong outlook and value system. We worked hard, appreciated what we had, supported each other, visited with our neighbours, read books, discussed everything, and learned as much as we could about the wider world.

A special treat was to go to the Fox's General Store at Regent for the mail and enjoy a 5 cent Coke or an ice cream cone. Sundays were community days. After the United Church services the kids would play while the grownups gossiped or discussed the weather. We drove over to Deloraine on Saturdays to shop and get the news. Deloraine was a 17 mile drive from the Browns' farm and unlike Hathaway and Regent it was big enough to be located in the *National Geographic Atlas*. We went to the Community Hall in Regent for social gatherings and dances, played baseball in the summer, and curled in the winter. A local farmer named Raymond Hodgson got the kids involved in the Regent 4H Calf Club. We had many good times together at 4H outings, but the highlight was selling the calves at the conclusion of the Boissevain Spring Fair each May. I knew then I was not going to be a farmer. Most of the kids were sad and cried seeing their beloved "pets" get sold at the final auction. To me it was a welcome relief to hear the auctioneer yell "Sold!" I was finally free of looking after a bloody calf, at least for the summer holidays.

Fortunately, Auntie was very education-oriented and since I was a bright eager student, she pushed me to do my best. There was no upper limit to what I could aspire or accomplish, and every new achievement was applauded with unconditional love. I never questioned what I was going to do after high school but rather what I was going to do after one or two university degrees. After a life in business I now have a full appreciation of Auntie's skill in subtly shaping my world-view. In sales we have a term called the assumptive close. One does not ask, "Are you considering purchasing a vehicle?" Instead, one assumes, "What colour would you like your new car to be, sir?" Well Auntie used that method on me with schooling and it worked so well that Anne and I have since used the assumptive close approach with our own daughters' education to great success. Collectively, Lydia and Jillian have achieved no less than eight university degrees, four apiece.

Auntie was a very clever lady, and I am indebted to her for much of who I am. Her affection and guidance anchored me in those undetermined and formative years. The Browns had only a small library at home, which was supplemented on a monthly basis by a provincial mail order borrowing library. Every month we ordered five new books to read and discuss before we sent them back. My monthly selections were subject to some censorship, mostly to broaden my horizons and reduce racy literature for a young fellow, but occasionally I managed to order *From Here to Eternity* or *Sons and Lovers* without getting caught out. I loved adventure stories, sea stories, and history books, and of course at least two of the five books in each order had to be classical literature to satisfy The Aunt. Every Saturday morning during the winter and spring we sat in the kitchen by the radio and listened to "Texaco at the Opera," which broadcast matinee performances of the Metropolitan Opera in New York. I am so grateful for that classical music upbringing now.

I have not mentioned Uncle very much, yet he was an incredibly important father figure and mentor. He was a gentle, unruffled man who usually deferred to The Aunt on big strategic decisions. Hard working, incredibly kind, Unc always saw the sunny side of a problem and no matter how frustrated he might get (or I might make him) I never heard him utter anything more damaging than "darn." He would have a quiet chuckle at some farm predicament or situation that had most of the other men stomping around in a rage. At family gatherings he would be in talking with the womenfolk instead of playing poker in the bunkhouse or standing around in the yard looking under the hood of the latest Oldsmobile Starfire V8. He had no need for bravado. Uncle taught me respect for all living things, he was a nurturer and a giver rather than a taker. Although he loved "Hockey Night in Canada," he helped me rationalize my complete lack of interest in television, hockey, and other professional sports, which persists to this day. I am sure I am one of only ten men in Canada who would not go across the street to watch an overpaid Canucks goons' game. But I never felt I had to justify going my own way. He loved me unconditionally. Uncle Alex was my biggest supporter and I just know I have made him proud.

After grade eight at Coxworth, I went to Dand High School, six miles west of home. To get to school I hitched a ride with Alf Horn in his black 1928 Model A Ford (it is easy to remember that it was black because all Model A Fords were black, a car with coloured paintwork came later). With its tall skinny tires, it could best any road condition: thick gumbo mud, snow drifts, or 40 below temperatures. My best accomplishment in high school was impressing a very pretty classmate named Anne Franklin as to our future possibilities when we both graduated and left our farms. She was very intelligent and as spirited as they come. We tried to impress and outperform each other in class: she got higher marks in the arts subjects while I occasionally managed to best her in the sciences. We were great friends, the intellectual competition was always keen, and she was undeterred by my impish ways. She would be with me every step as the story of my adult life unfolded.

When I count my blessings, I count her at least twice.

I went off to the University of Manitoba in Brandon in the fall of 1962 and by the fall of 1963 the Browns, by then in their late 60s, sold their farm and retired to Boissevain. An era had ended. Alex had been born on the property in 1894, a decade after his parents had settled there, among a first wave of mostly Ontario farmers of British ancestry who settled in the Regent area. The old Brown homestead site, on a small hill about half a mile from the current farmhouse, still had some trees around it and a wild asparagus patch. The most intriguing remnant was a depression in the ground about 12 by 15 feet which marked the site of the original "sod" house erected during their first few years of homesteading. Dug down about four feet, the thick sod walls were built up another four feet, topped by close-set log rafters to span the interior and a thick roof of sod above that. The dense layers of earth would provide good insulation in winter, but this one-room "root cellar" must have defined a very primitive existence.

Locals do not call Manitoba and Saskatchewan the "bald assed prairies" for nothing. No serious trees grew anywhere. That made it easy for farm clearing but a major challenge to obtain wood for fires and to build the houses and outbuildings. Fortunately, the well-wooded Turtle Mountains were about 20 miles to the south and in the winter months when Whitewater Lake was frozen over, the farmers became loggers. They cut wood on the mountain and dragged the logs home across the ice on horse-drawn sleighs and "stone-boats." The wood problem would be solved when the railway came to the prairies and milled construction lumber (for those who could afford to buy it) was shipped west from Ontario.

Genealogy

I come from pretty humble stock. The few genealogical documents I have include job descriptions for my ancestors that are wonderful in their modesty and obsolescence. My paternal grandfather James Taylor, his wife Amelia and their three kids, immigrated to Canada from Alloa, Scotland in 1912. I have traced the family roots back to at least the 1700s in that same area, near the mouth of the River Forth, east of Sterling. James owned a green-grocery store in Alloa and he listed his occupation on my dad's birth certificate as "coster." My father Thomas was born on June 1, 1905 at Murdostoun Castle, Scotland where James had moved on to work as a "gamekeeper." Once the family had settled in Ontario, my father worked first as a labourer in the logging industry and later, alongside his father, at the pulp and paper mill in Fort Frances. On their marriage certificate—dated April 22, 1932—my father, age 26, described his occupation as "wood piler" (which affords my daughters endless mirth). My mother, Florence Byzewski, at the age of only 18, was listed as a "spinster."

My mother's family had immigrated to Minnesota in the late 1870s from Danzig, Prussia, and settled on farms in the Granite Falls area. My maternal grandfather Joseph Byzewski was born in St. Cloud Minnesota and moved north with his wife Clarabelle to the Fort Frances area where he worked as a trapper and then as a section hand on the CN Railway in the little hamlet of Farrington. Mother was born there on June 19, 1913 at home with a midwife supervising. She had 7 siblings. Of my four grandparents, only Clarabelle was alive when I came along.

I was born in Fort Frances, Ontario, on September 7, 1944, the fifth child of Thomas and Florence Taylor. There were four children born before me and four more after me, oh our poor dear long-suffering mother. My siblings in descending age are Thomas *(February 4, 1933—July 27, 2020)*, Audrey *(December 8, 1934—January 26, 2006)*, Pearl *(November 10, 1936)*, Bob *(January 17, 1939—June 16, 2019)*, Richard *(September 19, 1947—December 5, 2020)*, Florence *(October 23, 1949)*, Cheryl *(March 15, 1952)*, and Debbie *(March 11, 1955)*. There were lots of adventures associated with our life in Farrington, where we lived after 1948, but one that stands out for me has to do with the arrival of a new sibling. There were no phones at home, so our only means of communication and transportation was the train that ran nearby several times a day. During daylight hours, one could put up a flag to signal to the engineer to stop the train, but at night it was a much bigger issue. The CNR had given our family a supply of "torpedoes" for emergencies. These were little detonators that could be affixed to the surface of the rail; when the passing train ran over the device it exploded with a huge bang, alerting the engineer to throw on the brakes.

I remember one night in March of 1952 when our mother went into labour. Complications arose after Cheryl was born, and we had to get mother and baby to Fort Frances hospital as soon as possible. A railway torpedo was placed on the track behind the house and sometime later in the night there was a loud bang and a screech of brakes as the train locked its wheels and shuddered to an emergency stop. Mom, Dad and baby Cheryl were bundled up, loaded into the caboose at the back of the train and away they went into town. Thankfully everyone was fine.

Anne and I were married in Deloraine on June 10, 1967, and we honeymooned at Expo 67 in Montreal. We have two daughters, Lydia born May 15, 1973, and Jillian born October 16, 1974, both in Vancouver, where no torpedoes were needed. We have four wonderful grandchildren: Lydia and Juan's Matias *(August 26, 2005)* and Taya *(August 12, 2007)*, and Jillian and Adam's Sophie *(October 26, 2006)* and Ian *(August 19, 2008)*. They are our future.

BELOW *My parents, Florence and Thomas Taylor, relaxing by their car near Fort Frances ON.*

RIGHT *Alex and Winnifred Brown on their wedding day, November 26, 1926.*

LEFT *Mitch after his triumph at the Brandon 4H calf scramble.*

BELOW *The four Taylor brothers dressed for Bob's wedding: Richard, Mitch, Bob and Tom.*

BELOW *My younger sisters, Debra, Cheryl, Florence, with my Mom, Mitch (kneeling), Dad and brother Richard.*

RIGHT *The Browns, Uncle and Auntie, at their house door in Boissevain MB.*

Impish Ways
Hypnotized Chickens
And Other Shocks

I may have wondered at eight or nine years old just what kind of character traits I was going to develop on my way to adulthood. I don't think anyone was worried that I might lack a sense of humour. Here are a few examples that will give you an inkling of what was to come.

In my study of the farmyard animals, I had determined that chickens were not very smart, in fact they are the dumbest animal of all. They do all sorts of stupid things. For example, all the silly birds would try to pile on to the same roost when it was obvious that the chosen roost was already full and a vacant one was waiting right beside it. Or take the feeding trough: if you filled two troughs with grain or kitchen scraps, every chicken would attempt to eat from only one of them. They would fight and squabble amongst themselves until all the food was spilled on the ground. Then they would rush off to the second trough and repeat the process. See, no brains, right?

Well, here is one trick I discovered that the dim-witted chickens could perform with little effort, in fact they could excel at it. They could be hypnotized.

If you draw a straight line in the sand, catch a chicken, soothe it a little and then stretch out its body on the ground, arranging its head so that one eye looks straight down that line, the dumb chicken will just lay there, forever theoretically, dreaming about what is at the end of that line, or something equally mesmerizing. I kid you not, I told you they are not very smart. I could get a dozen or more bird brains gazing intently at lines drawn all over the yard.

After I had amazed Auntie and Unc with my cleverness, I turned my hypnotizing skills into a game of chance by taking nickel bets from school friends or visitors to the farm. I wouldn't show them the trick. I would just profess great powers of chicken hypnosis, negotiate the bet, and then excuse myself for ten minutes to set up the gig. Seeing the amazing constellation of immobile creatures, most of my marks would think I had done the poor things in, gassed them or perhaps used decoy chickens, or whatever. Junior P.T. Barnum would then astound them anew by walking amongst the chickens and using the toe of his boot to gently push their bodies away from the fixated alignment. The dazed chickens would get up, shake their heads, stagger about a bit and then run off squawking to hide under the caragana hedges. I'd collect the doubters' bets and try not to look too chuffed. If I had more friends, I could have been rich.

One victim who needed to be set up with a certain amount of finesse was Ross St. John, Unc's nephew and in due course my favourite cousin. I looked up to Ross with intense admiration, but I had a burning need to best him at a game of chance or battle of wits. So far in our relationship I could not beat him at anything. He could outshoot me at crokinole, he could outguess me at hangman, he could pull a win out of checkers or Chinese checkers with only two pieces left, and he could whip me at cribbage. He was totally unbeatable. Of course, I hated to lose. It drove me crazy. The madder I got the more Ross laughed. Oooooh, he was just so infuriating. When I was not playing games with him, I loved him unconditionally. Ross was my hero, and a cherished friend. About 15 years older than me, he lived in Winnipeg with his girlfriend Gwen and he was a handsome steward on Air Canada, flying in Viscounts and Super Constellations across the country every day. His life seemed all so glamorous.

I badly needed a win, and my bird brain chickens were going to deliver the clincher. For weeks in advance I worked on "the setup." I told him I could hypnotize a chicken and he laughed me off. I pretended not to be offended. He challenged me to show him a hypnotized chicken. I demurred but still kept boasting tangentially that I could do it. Unc just smiled when he overheard the incessant banter. Finally, I ventured, "How much do you want to bet me that I can't?" Ross took the bait, "Five cents," he said dismissively. I pretended to weigh the matter. "OK," I said, "Five cents—per chicken, then." "You're on" was his reply, and with that the sting was underway. I ran down to the chickenyard, drew a hasty pattern in the dirt and lined up at least twenty birds with their heads to the ground. I blindfolded Ross and led him to the yard. He was absolutely flabbergasted. He could not believe his eyes. We watched for some minutes to prove the birds were transfixed, but eventually I had to go around and rouse every bird to prove they were still alive. Ross was a good sport, he paid up his dollar and with that I was no longer a little boy. Mitchie had come of age, he was now a force to be reckoned with.

Another trick that I was unable to monetize but still a source of endless mirth, was one involving the mechanism of an old telephone receiver. In those days the single telephone in our home was a wooden box hanging on the wall in the hall or kitchen. On the front of it was a mouthpiece speaker that you talked into and on the side of the box a bell-shaped receiver on a three-foot cord that you placed up against your ear. Below the earpiece mount there was a protruding crank connected to a magneto inside the box that you wound round and round to make an electric current go through the wires out of the house, down the road, and into the next farm or on to the switchboard in the nearest town (in our case Deloraine). The electric current would light up a little bulb on the switchboard and a lady named Daisy or May (they were sisters) would plug her own earphone into the socket by our light and ask what we wanted. You could give her the number of someone you wished to speak to locally, or she would connect you to a bigger switchboard like Brandon if you wanted to talk to someone a long distance away. Because our "party line" was shared with maybe ten neighbours, each home telephone had a distinctive call sign. Ours was two long rings and three short ones. To reach us you picked up your earphone to open the line, listened to see if anyone else was on it already, then turned the crank two long spins plus three short spins. We would hear that ring from the bell mounted on the top of the box and go pick up our receiver. If you heard someone else's number, you just ignored it. Or if the ringing went on too long you would pick up and say, "Sorry Mabel, they are not home, we saw them driving towards town after breakfast." It all sounds a bit more complicated than an iphone but it wasn't very hard to get on to.

Now back to my story. For some reason we had in our basement a spare magneto and the crank and a few other accessories for one of those phone sets, all disassembled. Being an inquisitive young engineer, I had to experiment with the ability of such a magneto to make an electric current, indeed a current of probably 50 volts DC. It was able to deliver a nice little shock if you held both sets of wires in your bare hands, thus completing the circuit. You can see where this is going, but I embellished the scenario a bit so my marks wouldn't figure out the trick too soon. We played a game called telephone. I convinced an amenable playmate to hold on to the mouthpiece with one hand (this connected to one wire) and then to hold on to the earpiece with the second hand (of course connected to the second wire). While he waited there, I pretended to ring him up, turning the crank so we could have a wee chat on the phone. It always worked like a charm. The caller's shrill screeches of alarm were almost drowned out by loud guffaws from the attending engineer, who would then apologize for wiring it up improperly. If the victim was too trusting or indeed gullible enough, I might even get a second scream before that game ended. The Aunt was never amused.

Another naughty trick that was only possible to play on male participants was a game called, "Let's pee over the fence." It was often initiated as a challenge to a visiting friend accompanied by a boast that I could pee higher than he could. I can't remember a boy under 14 who didn't take up the challenge, at least once. It is amazing how the penis competition begins at such an early age.

I have to admit that this game also involved electrical current, I guess I should have gone into electrical engineering. Most farms had places, like the garden plot or sometimes all the house lawns and gardens, that the owners didn't want the livestock to stray into. To secure these areas you could set up an electric fence, stringing a single wire along the top of a wood or wire fence. The electric wire was attached to the wood posts with insulators so that the charge would only stay in the wire until some creature came along and touched it, thus providing a ground for the current and delivering a shock to that grounding body. The shock was not very strong, but animals soon learned not to reach over that fence to nibble at the lettuce or geraniums. The shock was produced by a little transformer device we plugged into a barn's 120V outlet, located some distance away from the gardens.

Little boys like to pee on every possible thing and being generally competitive they can be easily double dared into peeing over a fence to prove they are "man" enough to do so. What most little boys do not know is that urine is very salty, salty water conducts electricity, and a stream of pee splashing on the electric fence connects the boy simultaneously to the fence and to the ground, completing a circuit that produces quite an amazing jolt to the young man's vulnerable dangly bits.

All I can say now to those trusting young men is that I am very sorry I took advantage of you. It did seem like such a clever trick at the time though, and an amusing use of the limited materials I had at hand. Tee hee.

A Sincere Apology

"Mr. Leuthwaite, I have something here that does not belong to me. I am giving it back to you now." The words were uttered softly, deliberately, with heavy resignation.

I shifted nervously from foot to foot as I faced the sales counter in the local hardware store. Mr. Leuthwaite towered behind it, his palms resting on the glass surface.

The Aunt, my moral compass and guardian, was standing just a few feet behind me, listening intently to my carefully scripted words. Like my heroes in the Zane Grey cowboy novels, my back was against the wall, this room was now high noon and I had one chance left to regain my dignity. There was no way out.

The big railway clock on the wall behind Mr. Leuthwaite stopped ticking.

In those days most rural boys owned a small caliber long gun; mine was a single shot Winchester 22 rifle. Its authorized purpose was to shoot pesky gophers, to prevent them from digging dangerous burrows in the fields near the cattle water holes. City kids might have a difficult time grasping how gopher holes could be dangerous, but the cattle could be injured if they stumbled on uneven ground, and a cow with a broken ankle was a dead cow. In my mind my Winchester was a prized model 74 lever-action 30-30 carbine that instantly took me from the slow paced farm life in Manitoba to the endless rolling hills of my imaginary cowboy ranch in Montana. As I rode my mighty steed around the ranch I might often catch and dispense justice to an evil band of cattle rustlers.

The Aunt had found a new box of bullets in my bedroom that morning. She knew that my meager allowance could not have covered their cost and that maybe, just maybe, I had obtained those bullets through improper means. After several futile attempts at denial, I tearfully confessed to stealing them. Now that the interrogation was over, my last hope for personal salvation was that The Aunt might go visit Mr. Leuthwaite, resolve the issue, and all would return to normal.

I was totally wrong. There was only one possible resolution for this situation. Restitution in Person accompanied by a Sincere Apology with Eye Contact.

A Sincere Apology with Eye Contact was about the lowest, most degrading, humiliation this eleven year old boy could ever imagine. I would be ruined forever. I could never walk those streets again. I would have to run far away. My life as I knew it was over.

"You know young man, you did something very wrong, something you must never do again. You must learn a valuable lesson here. This experience will forever be a part of who you are as a man. Being able to say you are sorry is a vital lesson for life. One day you will appreciate that," the Aunt reassured me.

The big clock on the wall above the counter would not tick forward. Sweat beaded my forehead yet my hands felt cold and clammy. My brain churned over and over. I stole a look back. Auntie smiled a little "go on" encouragement. I loved my Auntie very much and I knew she loved me.

I mustered my courage and turned to look at Mr. Leuthwaite. My eyes met his. The clock ticked.

"I am very sorry for my behavior. I promise you both that I will never steal again."

He reached over the counter and gently took the package from my trembling hands. He set it aside and then he took my hands in his. His eyes found mine. "Thank you son, I believe in you."

That experience in the Leuthwaite Hardware Store was a life-altering one for me. I probably did not digest all the messages until some years later but if each experience gives a young man a pearl of wisdom, I came home with a necklace. Deloraine was a small close-knit community, everyone looked after everyone else, we were all our brothers' keepers. Mr. Leuthwaite cared as much for me and for my upbringing as did The Aunt. He could have responded in any number of ways and yet he took the very highest road in dealing with this incident. He chose the carrot of solidarity instead of the stick of righteousness. I learned how to say I was sorry, my life was not ruined, I was able to walk out of that store with my head held high and to know that, yes, I had made a mistake, but in resolving that mistake I had learned much more than just the obvious "Thou shalt not steal."

One of the insights was the realization that I belonged to a community. All of the people in it cared for me, believed in me, and not only supported me to succeed but expected me to do my best. That was a gift. One I also try to carry forward.

Auntie as usual had also taken a high road. She could have punished me in any number of ways, but she decided the character-building one of telling the truth, taking responsibility for my own actions, and dealing upfront with a situation was the better lesson. Neither she nor Unc ever mentioned that incident again, but then they didn't need to. I can tell you honestly that I never stole anything again.

A Calf Scramble Explained

I mentioned the Regent 4H Calf Club and our neighbour Raymond Hodgson who mentored us in the business of animal husbandry. In those days, if you were a kid who lived on a prairie farm you belonged to your community 4H club; it was like belonging to the Boy Scouts if you lived in a town or city. Both boys and girls were welcome. In bigger communities there would have been other 4H Clubs focused on Sewing or other activities but at Regent we only had a Calf Club. In addition to the business of looking after cattle we learned a lot of "future citizen" skills: service to the community, looking out for others, and being accountable for our actions. It was an early finishing school for farm kids.

As part of this polishing, we had to participate in a public speaking contest held every spring. Regrettably, that meant standing in front of a crowd of people and delivering a prepared speech for a few minutes. Two words come to mind: excruciating and painful. I have since described my early fear of public speaking in terms of an impossible choice, such as a choice between giving a public speech and walking into a burning building. Most of us would have chosen the latter if there had been any choice. There was no welching allowed. To prolong the agony, the event was set up as a province wide contest. We presented to our own clubs, the local winners would go to a series of regional contests and eventually, after many speeches and narrowing down of talents, the future Winston Churchill would be chosen to represent the province. I never did win the trophy but as if goaded by Lady Macbeth I did screw my courage to the sticking place and I did not fail. Over several years of speaking contests, I gained confidence and eventually overcame the next biggest fear which was wetting my pants.

When I was fifteen years old, I got invited to take part in a Labatt's sponsored Calf Scramble at the Brandon Winter Fair. The Calf Scramble capped a week-long agricultural fair which was held every spring on the Brandon Exhibition grounds. The big indoor stadium must have held at least 5000 spectators. Twenty boys aged 14 to 18 and ten calves were going to do a rodeo joust in the arena oval. The boys were lined up at one end of the arena and the calves were let in at the other. The object was to run down a calf and drag it over the finish line.

A Calf Scramble Explained

It was not that easy. Trying to outrun another teenager was one thing, trying to outrun a very spooked 300-pound calf was another. Tackling the bloody thing and then holding it down while tying a halter around its head and neck was a challenge too. Totally spent from all of that activity, the calf rustler still had to drag the weighty beast across the finish line, countering the resistance of its four legs all sticking straight out in total defiance. And did I mention there were twenty boys and only ten calves? That meant a certain amount of skill and cunning to keep your eye on the prize from the very beginning. Spoiler alert: I did it. I sprinted down the field like Roger Bannister, picked out a single beast when most of the other calves were still huddling together near the chute, and bested the little bugger. I flipped him off his feet, got the halter secured around its head after several frustrating attempts, and slowly but surely dragged him across the line. My main memory of that great adrenaline rush game was wondering whether I could maintain enough strength to drag that obstinate beast halfway across the stadium. Having practiced with a few thousand bales of hay each summer must have helped my arm muscles a little. But the excited roars of a packed stadium provided the biggest boost factor, especially because one of the greatest roarers of all was a young lady named Anne, sitting beside Auntie and Unc. How could I possibly lose?

Mister Labatt gave each winner $150 with which to buy a beef steer to train and fatten up for the next 4H season or to sell at the next Brandon Winter Fair. Thankfully Raymond Hodgson, who maintained a herd of purebred Hereford cattle, stepped in and gave me some excellent advice. "Forget about buying a steer to fatten up for sale. Take your $150 win and buy two certified purebred heifers. Raise them to be breeding stock, not steaks, and in a few years' time you will have lots of steers and heifers for sale."

It was like turning on a money machine. Raymond and I went to a fall cattle sale in Saskatchewan and brought home two lovely little Hereford heifers. Jump forward three or four years to when the Browns decided to sell their farm and retire to Boissevain, and I was able to sell 9 or 10 head of cattle. Counting the cash that day was as close as I would come to becoming a farmer, plus it was a very welcome addition to my university education fund.

— 2 —

ODD JOBS

I've had a lot of jobs. Some more odd than others. In the early days they were odd in the sense of various and diverse, as I took what I could get to earn money based on what was available at the time to a young person who was strong, willing, and not yet an expert at anything. Strenuous physical labour featured centrally. These are some of the jobs I had before I graduated from university in 1965.

Because I loved school and had no passion for farming, from an early age I was determined to go to university. My adolescent dream fixated on medicine because doctors were the most learned and respected people in the local community. I applied to pursue a Bachelor of Science at the University of Manitoba in Brandon; it was a well-regarded school, close to home (so I could continue to visit and look after the Browns), and cheaper than a leap to the University of Toronto or UBC, which I mentally kept in reserve with hopes to continue on to medical school. I may also have been influenced by the fact that the striking Anne Franklin chose the U of M for her Bachelor of Arts studies. The Browns cheered me on but did not have extra money to support my studies at university. Throughout high school and university, I worked hard to fill the coffers to pay for tuition and living expenses. Fortunately, I managed to reel in several merit scholarships and bursaries for the top students (Auntie told me I was too clever by half). I paid the rest of my way through hardscrabble summer jobs and by living as frugally as possible, which was not hard to do since I had been practicing frugality from birth.

Farm hand

As a kid, from my arrival at the Browns through high school, I worked on our own farm doing whatever a farm boy needs to do. This included milking cows; separating the cream from the milk in the cream separator; feeding the animals; cleaning the manure out of the barn and spreading it on the fields or heaving it on the manure pile out behind the trees; fixing the barb wire fences all around the property; maintaining and painting the buildings and sheds; fixing the machinery, including engine repairs on the tractor, combine, and family car; driving the tractor in the fields for seeding; cultivating the summer fallow; swathing the mature grain fields and combining at harvest time; bringing in grain wagons from the fields to the granaries; using pitchforks to put up loose hay onto a big wheeled rack pulled by horses and loading it into the capacious loft of the barn with overhead slings (the hay was for feeding the cattle in the winter); mowing the lawns in the farmyard; helping with dishes and cleaning in the house;

and weeding in the garden. All this was rather demanding, but it provided an astonishingly broad skill set for tackling most situations in life, from basic survival skills to carpentry, mechanics, and the odd Apollo-13 type engineering challenge.

From age fourteen through seventeen I also worked for our neighbour Raymond Hodgson, at something like sixty dollars for the season (from late spring into early summer) baling hay for a large herd (300 plus) of purebred Hereford cattle. Raymond would have already swathed the fields of alfalfa and other grasses and after the mown stalks lay drying in the sunshine for a few days, we came along with a tractor-drawn baler towing a big flat rack. The baler bundled up the grasses, compressed each lot into a heavy rectangle, tied it together with binder twine, and pushed the finished bale of hay out a chute onto the rack behind. Standing on that moving rack behind the baler as it wound around the field, my job was to grab each emerging bale with a meat-hook type tool, heave the bale to the back of the rack and stack it neatly in dense interlocking rows. Depending on the speed of the tractor and the density of the swath, the bales came off the baler at a furious rate, most times requiring two people on the rack to handle the volume. It was hot, sweaty, back-breaking work, especially as the load got higher and higher. Each bale weighed around thirty pounds. To stack bales on the higher levels you had to grab the bale off the chute by the twine bindings, twist around with it and throw it up several levels in one continuous movement. The upper elf[1] would then fit the bale into the matrix until the load was at least five or

---

[1] In the nomenclature of our household devised by Lydia and Jillian one Christmas, the upper elf is a person who performs any job requiring greater height or dignity, while the lower elf ends up crawling around on their knees completing the less desirable tasks.

six levels high. After a couple of weeks of this intense activity our arms and shoulders were awesome, a great source of pride at the swimming hole, tee hee. A season of haying could mean handling 20,000 bales twice (heaving them onto the rack in the field and then stacking them in the hay loft or farmyard).

Smelter sweeper in a nickel mine

After first year of university concluded in May 1963, those of us who had to make serious money for the next year's tuition went in search of the highest paying jobs we could find. A few of us—Marsh Kennedy, Phil North, Don McLaren, Cyril Fox and I—decided to go north to Thompson in Northern Manitoba, way north. We drove Marsh's 1950 Ford sedan to The Pas and caught a train from there to Thompson, a classic company mining town, built around an International Nickel Company of Canada (INCO) mine. I think it was the second largest nickel mine in the world, the site of vast underground excavating and the smelting and refining of some 40,000 tons of nickel per year. The Crawley Camp at the mine site for the workers housed over 3500 people but after enduring a week there we decided to rent an apartment in the town about five miles away. We could get to and from work by company bus, but sometimes if weather permitted, we jogged home after our shifts. We rented a bachelor apartment in the Pink Apartments where the sleeping arrangement was five air mattresses laid out parallel to each other about a foot apart. (A navy man would have nodded at the close quarters which resembled the crowded hammocks in an old sailing man o' war). We all took a medical exam which Phil failed due to his poor eyesight, so he headed back home. We were sad to see him go but we soon found a new body, named Moss, to fill the vacancy in the Pink Apartments.

At the INCO site there were positions open for underground (the highest paid), smelter, and refinery. Marsh and Cyril chose to go underground but I chose the smelter position because I had no interest in the possibility of getting stuck several thousand feet beneath the surface of the earth (no one did of course). I soon found out the smelter position was not such a smart choice either, health-wise. Every workday I spent hours sweeping the ever-present nickel dust off the floors and furnaces and returning that valuable detritus to the smelting furnaces. I am talking about two inches of dust accumulation each day over several acres of the smelter's floors. Our sweeping crew might number two dozen men, all Newbies or Newfies it seemed. Newbies (like me) were the lowest level of humanity and treated as such. Newfies, our unfairly badgered brethren from Newfoundland, fared only slightly better. A fortune in nickel was salvaged each day, during which time a dangerous amount of poisonous gas and particulate got into our unprotected throats and noses. Dust masks were for pussies.

Sweeping off the massive electric-fired furnaces was the trickiest part, and incredibly dangerous. The all-brick furnaces were approximately forty feet wide, two hundred feet long, and sixty feet tall. Down the middle of each furnace ran several six-foot diameter pipes (the electrodes) filled with big chunks of carbon which would arc against the metal at the bottom of the furnace at maybe 1400 degrees Celsius to liquefy the nickel concentrate. The rooves of the furnaces were also made of brick and were domed like a Florentine church so that they were structurally sound. The soundness did not extend to our approach though, because we had to lay planks across the curved brick surface and attach a safety line to an overhead building beam just in case the furnace roof caved in while we were sweeping it. I witnessed several instances when a brick would be dislodged and fall into the boiling caldron far below. At night I dreamt of the whole furnace roof giving way and Mitchie hanging there like a marionette on his paltry lifeline over the 1400-degree liquid nickel bubbling below. Fortunately, I survived that summer and happily pocketed my $2 per hour pay cheques. I had no problem with the concept that a university degree was going to be a better outcome than a promotion to INCO shift boss. I earned enough money to pay for tuition, and in second year I spent a little bit more time studying and a little less time playing Bridge.

Welder's helper on a pipeline

For the next year's summer job, Cyril, Phil and I landed jobs on the Trans Canada natural gas pipeline which was being constructed from Alberta to Ontario in the early 1960s, taking natural gas to the markets in eastern Canada and the US. I was lucky enough to get a job as a welder's helper working with a senior welder doing roving repairs along the line. The construction of a pipeline—much like the laying of a rail line—was a complicated series of precise, consecutive steps that unfolded as the project crawled like a millipede across the prairies. Surveyors laid out the predetermined route; bulldozers and grading machines cleared the right of way of any trees, small hills, or other obstacles; trenching machines came along and dug a ditch six feet wide and ten feet deep, piling all the dirt to the left of their travel; a convoy of semi-trailer trucks followed, each delivering five 80-foot sections of

36-inch steel pipe and setting them end to end on wooden trestles alongside the open trench. Approximately ten miles behind this segment came a group of Caterpillar 583 pipelayers, welding machines on trucks or carts, countless support vehicles and several busloads of workers. Each section of pipe needed to be carefully welded together, wrapped with insulation, laid into the ditch and covered over.

The pipe welding process required two rounds of welding by four welders for each joint, working in pairs with one positioned on either side of the pipe. The first two welders did a hot-pass, laying down a thin bead of liquid iron to connect the pipes at the innermost point in the V sloped edge of the joints. The second pair followed and carefully filled in the rest of the V, capping it on the outside with a slightly raised braid of metal, which had to form a perfect weld. Because the second pass required at least four times as much time to complete as the first hot-pass, there were four to six sets of these welding duos leapfrogging each other as the process moved forward. The Caterpillar pipelayers had an adjustable boom that reached out and held the pipe in a sling. Several pipelayers in a row held up the finished pipe and several more brought in new sections to be added. Because safety was essential in a high-pressure gas pipeline that needed to operate for many decades to come, our welds had to be 100% perfect every time. To ensure that level of excellence, a radioactive x-ray photograph was taken of each weld and delivered to a mobile developing lab where it was approved or rejected by a Trans Canada Pipelines Inspector. Mistakes were made of course because hangovers were prevalent and even the tiniest piece of slag in the weld would trigger a rejection. A big yellow crayon X would be marked on the offending section of pipe.

After each section of line was finished, approved, and wrapped with insulation, the pipelayers would come along and drop it into the ditch, followed by the backfill bulldozers and the landscapers. We completed as much as four miles a day of finished pipeline that summer across the flat prairies, I think a record only surpassed in Texas. We worked seven days a week, often from dawn to dusk, and dusk came late to our northern jobsites in summer. We lived in motels in towns close to the right of way or we camped out in a tent when the construction moved east between Leader, Swift Current, and Regina. I made pretty good money because although we were only earning $2.50 an hour, we could get massive overtime and double overtime cheques.

My final summer job at university involved working for a second year on the same pipeline with the same welder. I was the designated peon (lower elf) for a hot shot welder from Saskatoon, a gruff man in his late 20s named Don. He had his own rig: a shiny blue Ford F350 flatbed equipped with a powerful V8, the latest welding machine and custom cabinets. Don's outsized ego matched his rig. He had finished at the top of the ratings on his initial hiring-on welding test and could have whatever position he wanted. He picked the "tie-in" crew. Our truck was on radio call alert to fix any problem that might hold up putting the newly welded pipe into the ground. Most of the time that meant visiting the Mobile X-ray Inspection Trailer with its yellow radioactive triangle on the wall and picking up a daily report of the welds that were rejected that day. There were two kinds of repairs required: inside the pipe there were "burn thru's" which happened at the hot-pass stage, and on the outside of the pipe there might be "slag" in the weld, or QC issues with the "braid" on the outer seam. Due to the upside-down position a welder needed to take to make the weld on the underside of the pipe, the majority of imperfections occurred in the bottom section, which was the most difficult to repair for the same reason.

A welder's helper did everything there was to do with the job description of both he and his welder, except for the welding part. That may sound a bit self-important but it was true. The welders made big money; they were the top of the profession. In contrast to my $2.50, Don made $30 an hour plus another $25 an hour for supplying his own truck and equipment. Don was a prima donna, ergo, here is a standard day for me. Wake up about 4 a.m. to tackle the first two jobs of the morning, which I took on for extra money. I would run out to the parked company vehicles, start each one up, slide across the seat and out the passenger door, leap into the next one and start it too, and on through the long line. Then I'd go back in reverse order, checking to make sure the engines were running and restarting any that had stalled. When every truck was running, I would jump in a flatbed stake-sided truck filled with igloo water coolers and dash off to the closest ice storage place, fill the coolers with shovels full of ice, turn a hose on them until they were full, clap on their caps and rush back to the equipment yard. Every piece of equipment had to have an ice-cold drinking water cooler in its holder before the union worker would deign to walk near it. Temperatures on the prairies in the summer could easily be 100 degrees F, so I don't blame them. Then I would dash back to the trucks and turn off the warm engines. That little exercise which I could generally accomplish at high speed in under two hours brought me two x four hours of pay before I even started my day job at 6 a.m., now fully on overtime pay for eight hours with double overtime after that.

I'd head back to the motel to pick up Don, who was probably still drunk or had cuts to bandage from the latest fight, load him into the truck and drive off to the work site, stopping for coffee and a donut on the way. The drive could be up to forty miles away. I got to drive while Don would sleep and recover his steady welding arm and hopefully, sober up. First order of the day was the Inspection trailer where I would look over all the film from the last x-ray run, take note of where the repairs had to be made (inside or outside the pipe, right or left side, distance from the top or bottom) and on which weld number (all marked on the outside of the pipe). For the outside repairs, with Don usually still asleep, I would drive the truck up the line, mark each spot needing repair using a tape measure and a yellow marker, then turn the rig around at the repair closest to the front and get to work. Crank up the welding machine on the back of the truck, take out a big metal grinder, put on a face shield and proceed to carefully grind out the imperfection so that Don could fill in the repair spot. Repairs underneath the pipe meant lying on your back in the dirt and wriggling into position before grinding. It was hot and dirty and little pieces of metal coming off the grinder would burn any exposed skin, often right through your tee shirt. Then I would attach the ground wire to the pipe, unroll enough heavy cable to get to the site, get Don's helmet ready, prepare a supply of welding rods, and go wake the Prince of the Weld.

Remember, Don only wielded the stinger, nothing else. He would come along and weld up the join I had prepared, I would grind off any slag, and he would cap the weld. Then he went back to the truck while I tidied up the finished repair with a stiff wire brush on a second grinder, loaded the equipment, moved the truck to the next repair site and started again. Our repairs had to be 100% perfect every time. If you made a mistake the pipe could not be buried, and we would be "run off" or fired for holding up the line. Don was good, even semi drunk and in a foul temper. I do not ever remember a single rejection.

If the repairs needed to be done on the inside of the pipe, that was a whole new proposition. I would back the truck up to the open pipe which was hopefully on trestles only a foot or so off the ground. I placed a little cart in the pipe, a platform made from a section of pipe itself, about one-foot square with four roller bearings welded on each corner for the wheels. I'd hook the end of the welding stinger to the cart, crawl onto the cart on my knees and go scooting off inside the pipe, pulling the stinger and its trailing cable with me. The heavy welding cable must have been 5/8 of an inch thick but with strong legs I could usually drag it in about five or six pipe lengths (carefully counting the clicks as the wheels ran over each pipe joint—essential because I had to know how many clicks to the furthest repair). When my strength ran out, I needed to turn around, sit down inside the pipe cross-legged and pull in another section of cable. I would go to the furthest point, deposit the stinger there and start back, counting each click and marking the repair spots, nearly always at the bottom. Then I'd scurry back to the opening and send in Don, cruising to the endpoint with his flashlight and his welding rods. A shout of OK from the pipe and I would pull him back to the next repair, retracting his bulk on the cart by winding up the cable on a big windlass on the back of the truck. He weighed at least 230 pounds, it was not an easy job but again, very good for building strong arms and shoulders.

Some days were easier than others. The welders were all young men who drank themselves silly on Friday and Saturday nights, so most repairs were from welds attempted early on their mornings-after. Some weekdays there would be only a few repairs and we could sit in the shade, drink coffee or ice water and veg out until the radio squawked over the loudspeaker or the Inspection trailer called with a new round of results. By the end of August I felt like I deserved a medal. Instead, I happily went back to university with enough money in the bank to pay off my loans, cover my fourth-year tuition and living costs, and still finance a trip to Europe in the winter of 1965.

ODD JOBS

BELOW *Go-Kart racing in Thompson MB, 1963.*

BELOW *Mitch as a welder's helper on a pipeline job site in Saskatchewan.*

TOP RIGHT *Phil North and Mitch beside his 1953 Chevrolet, on the car ferry near Leader SK.*

BOTTOM RIGHT *Mitch sitting on a rock contemplating his future.*

FOLLOWING PAGE *Mitch, University of Manitoba, Class of 1965.*

FOLLOWING PAGE *Anne Franklin, University of Manitoba, Co-president of the student body, Class of 1965.*

ODD JOBS

Mitch with the Browns' 1961 Ford Falcon at their house in Boissevain MB.

— 3 —

THE OPEN ROAD &
THE CORPORATE LADDER

Much of my early life can be chronicled through cars. I understand this high octane obsession is anathema now in the age of alternative energy and looming environmental catastrophe. But an honest account of our experiences and dreams in the 1950s and 60s requires highlighting the automobile as both a fixture of life and a metaphor for our rapidly expanding horizons in the postwar boom. Cars meant individual freedom, independence, physical and social mobility, expanded opportunity for travel, and it seemed, for everything else one could dream of. With each new year the choice of automotive designs increased dramatically: they were bigger, better, faster, they came in more colours, they were ever more powerful (and carbon consumptive, though no one thought about it at the time). They mirrored the booming economic growth in our country and helped to link together its far-flung communities and outposts. For teenage boys, car-talk easily took up half of our conversations. We could identify every make and model, we knew every available option, and we were all aware of which neighbours had the most coveted vehicles. And we could not wait to be 16 years old so we could get a driver's license and speed off somewhere, anywhere actually, as long as we could get out on the open road.

My very first car was formerly the Browns' family car: an old blue two-tone 4-door 1949 Monarch with forward opening rear "suicide" doors and a great 255 cubic inch flathead V8. The car became mine after the Browns purchased a Ford Falcon. I drove the Monarch through first year of university but by then it was burning a quart of oil per tank of gas. In 1963 I sold it and bought a well-used 4-door 1953 Chevrolet Bel Air sedan, brown, with a 6 cylinder engine and a two speed powerglide automatic transmission. It became car number two and the first car I went out and paid for with my own money. It cost all of $150 actually. Certainly not the most powerful car on the block, the Bel Air was reliable transportation through my years at university. After graduation in 1965 I sold the Bel Air and went off on my first trip abroad, a seven month tour of Europe.

A Grand Tour on $5 a Day

Transportation in the UK and Europe was a mixed bag of low cost options. We were trying to live on $5 a day, which was actually quite "doable" as they say now. *Europe on $5 a Day* was the title of a popular travel guide at the time. Our crew of three—Phil North, Norm Reid, and Mitch Taylor—spent much of senior year planning this great adventure. We started out in Scotland with public transportation, but that did not work very well because it took too long to get from place to place. When we got to Belfast, Ireland, we each bought a bicycle and started pedaling our way around the beautiful green isle. A bike seemed like a good idea because you got to see a lot of country, you could stop at every pub or point of interest and it cost nothing to operate. Unfortunately, it soon dawned on us that we were not going to see enough of Europe at 15 miles an hour. Soon the bicycles were abandoned, and we were hitchhiking.

Three guys with backpacks was a hard sell for those small European cars—especially since Phil North, representing our Canadian "true north strong and free," had a pair of ice skates optimistically dangling from the outside of his backpack—so we decided the best way to travel was to split up for the journey and regroup at predetermined spots. I liked that idea best anyway. Tramping alone you got to meet new people with every pick up, you learned a lot about the country in a fairly short conversation, and the hidden gem was the fact that in Ireland, every driver wanted to talk, and drink beer, and that was best done via a stop in one of the countless cozy pubs along the road. I would often get a lift from one fellow in the morning, he would insist on stopping for a pint and a bite to eat. My "OK if you insist," and then at the pub, a neighbour's "Where are you headed?" might secure the next driver, some fellow seated nearby in the bar who would make the same generous offer of transportation and pub hospitality an hour or so later. Free beer, free food, free ride, lots of friendly banter and local knowledge, and sometimes even a free couch to sleep on. I met a lot of great people and learned a lot about the country that I might never have known otherwise.

The solo hitchhiking concept worked really well throughout Europe and although our pals saw less of each other en route we always reconvened in the bigger cities where we stayed at youth hostels. With no cell phones or any other means of communication we relied upon American Express (Amex) offices to leave messages for each other and to get messages from home. (Since we are Manitobans and our families expressed love through food, we sometimes found a package of homemade butter tarts or cookies waiting for us at an Amex office.) Generally, after arriving in a city we would check the Amex office every day until the others showed up, or if one couldn't wait he would leave a note indicating where next and move on out. Our general path led from the UK through the Low Countries, to France, Spain, Italy, Austria, Germany, Belgium, then back to the UK and home. Travelling independently was exactly what I was needing. I could spend hours and days in churches or castles or museums and no one would be impatiently waiting for me. As this was my first trip outside Canada (other than trips to nearby parts of the US) I had due reverence for the architecture and history to be soaked in. A humorous aside here is that I also got to learn a lot about scotch on that trip and was able to triumphantly write home to Auntie to announce, "You will be pleased to know that I have acquired a taste for scotch." Somehow, I doubt that she was pleased with that, being a teetotaler and always very critical of our uncles who drank. True to form she never said a disapproving word.

While living like kings on the beach in Marbella, Spain, and drinking scotch at less than $1 a bottle, we met some other travellers who were heading home and wanted to sell their car. On offer was an early 1950s 2-stroke German DKW, which was a tiny thing like a VW beetle made by the DKW company, one of several companies that eventually merged into Auto Union and then the Audi Group. To call that car an Audi predecessor would have been a stretch. It was a hopeless little car that we managed to purchase for $44. It had a constantly dead battery and a leak in the radiator requiring a 5 gallon refill pail by the driver's seat. It could not carry three large guys up a steep hill, so whenever we encountered an incline two of us would hop out and lope along until the driver crested the hill and everyone jumped back in again. One night I got stopped by the Italian highway patrol and was ordered off the freeway. We were going flat out but far too slow for their rules. The end came in later winter when we were in Venice preparing to leave for Vienna. The roads from this A to B went over the Alps, and the little DKW was deemed unfit for the task. There was no time to sell it and it was worth about as much as we had paid for it, which was next to nothing. I left it in the parking lot of a rest stop in Mestre and penned a note to lay face up on the dash, alongside the key:

> To Whom It May Concern, this car is yours for the taking, no strings attached, except the battery is dead. Enjoy your New Car.

After graduating from the University of Manitoba, Anne went on to UBC to study English and education while I went off on my great "continental tour" as any proper English boy might aspire to do. It really was a shame that she could not accompany me on that trip. In that era, society did not approve of unmarried couples traipsing around together, in Europe or anywhere else. And we were of course a very proper young couple with aspirations to move up into that society. Phil and Norm were good travel mates but Anne would have been a much better travel companion with her interest in art, history, literature and culture. Please do not fret though dear reader, you will find out that Miss Anne became an accomplished world traveller over the next five or six decades. When I was abroad in 1965 Anne and I kept in touch long distance and when my tour was over I went directly to Vancouver to visit her.

Birth of a Salesman

It was the summer of 1966. My initial plan was to find a summer job and then apply to medical school at UBC. I took on a succession of incredibly hard piece-meal jobs. One involved unloading fertilizer from box cars (don't ask me why they shipped fertilizer in a box car instead of a tank car) scooping it by the shovelful onto a conveyer belt. The boss came by at about 3 p.m. to see how I was doing. The car was empty, all 75 tons of cargo had been moved. He was flabbergasted. He said, "You'd better come into the executive offices with me and apply for a full time job. Do you realize that we usually have two guys on that job, and it takes them two full days? We could use your kind of talent upstairs, not down here, but that's your choice." Another job was shipping and receiving giant cases of Imperial Tobacco products in a warehouse. I knew that was a dead-end job for sure. So, with a wee twinge of consciousness, I went into Imperial Oil's head office in Vancouver and applied for a permanent position, not a summer job.

The managers I met were all very enthusiastic about Imperial Oil and its highly acclaimed career paths available to employees with university degrees. I was offered a job right away and signed on as an Industrial Sales Representative. On my way home I took the first step of my new career. I stopped at Chapman's Men's Wear to buy a couple of spiffy executive suits.

As an Industrial Sales Rep my job was to sell Imperial Oil's various fuel and lubrication products to industrial users. Given my science degree with a major in organic chemistry, I was a shoo-in for this position. It took no time to understand the oils, greases, and other products, I just needed to learn how to be a salesman. After six weeks in a sales training course for new recruits in the Toronto head office I knew how to do that too. I was sent off to a territory based in Kamloops, British Columbia, and assigned a well-used wine coloured 1964 Pontiac company car. Imperial Oil was a very conservative company, its public image was carefully scripted by decree, from cars to dress codes. Our company cars were all four door sedans of the lowest level of trim and colour and our field offices had to be modest and unremarkable. As to attire, like all other salespeople I wore a dark suit with a fresh white shirt and dark tie every day. I carried a leather briefcase with my name engraved on the lid, and I wore brown or black brogues all year long. I only owned socks of one colour, black (an ascetic habit I keep to this day, even outfitted for the gym).

Upon reflection, I must have looked pretty silly driving into a remote and dusty sawmill yard or a muddy mining show in my freshly pressed suit, tie, and white shirt, but that was the order of the day and no one ever kicked me off the property for being a candy ass. Imperial Oil happily paid for dry cleaning and car washes. A salesperson had to look the part as well as perform it. One of my bosses, Norm Ross, gave me great advice, which I tell everyone I have hired since. He said, "Mitch, you must try to never meet professionally with someone who is better dressed than you are, it looks bad for the company and reflects badly on you too. The best way for a businessman to dress is in a suit and tie and a crisp white shirt."

I travelled out into my territory nearly every week because the only way to meet my customers was to seek them out at their place of business. Unlike a city territory, my customers ranged over an area larger than the whole United Kingdom. I basically lived in my uncomfortable company car. Kamloops was my home base; my sales territory stretched from Alexis Creek in the west of the Chilcotin area, some 400 miles east to Valemount near the Rocky Mountains. If you drew my territory as a triangle, the southern tip would be Princeton near the US border. That meant I spent most of my time driving to see every major ranch, logging show, sawmill, mine, industrial or construction site in that vast terrain, putting at least 30,000 miles per year on the company car.

Unfortunately, my poor Pontiac came to an ignominious end when in late 1966 I was travelling up the new (construction-in-progress) Yellowhead Highway from Kamloops to Jasper and got mired down in thick mud on the partially constructed highway near Blue River. One of Peter Kiewit's D9 cats kindly attached a heavy chain to my bumper and slowly pulled me through the sludge so thick that it was soon piling up onto the hood. Then came a loud grinding sound of ripping metal and through the grubby windshield I saw the D9 lumbering away down the road with the bumper and most of the front end of my car still attached to his chain.

The mud mishap meant a chance to order my first brand new company car: a 1967 fire-engine red Ford Custom with a peppy 289 V8, the same engine powering those hot Shelby Mustangs of the era. I loved that car, which was a good thing because I basically lived in it. I did develop into a successful salesman and I had a little luck too because under my watch the huge open pit mines of Bethlehem Copper and Lornex got started and I was already in like Flynn in that area. Imperial Oil made many millions of dollars out of those contracts in the Highland Valley (and probably still does). Don't worry I do not claim credit, although I was most certainly involved in every diesel oil or lube oil aspect of all those early Highland Valley mines. My reputation as an up-and-coming star performer did not suffer in the halls of the head office either.

Anne and I got engaged at Christmas time in Kamloops in 1966 and we got married the next June 10 in Deloraine, Manitoba. After the church service we were proudly paraded around the little town in a horse buggy pulled by a modernized horse cum garden tractor, driven by a widely smiling friend Gerry Whetter. After our exciting honeymoon at the World's Fair, Expo 67 in Montreal, where we were inspired to see so many countries of the world coming together in such a positive and uplifting way, we settled into a new, somewhat bigger apartment upstairs from the bachelor pad I shared with Jim Gillis on Battle Street.

You'll read more about that inaptly named residence in the next section. We had lots of parties and made fantastic friends on Battle Street, like our neighbours Carol and Clive Schindler. I introduced myself to them by pulling pranks, like stealing the muddy shoes they left outside their door at night or stuffing the toes of their shoes with crumpled newspapers. Carol and Clive became our lifelong best friends; and if there were any battles between Anne and I, the Schindlers could be counted on to prop up both sides. We loved those years living in Kamloops. Along with the new friends we enjoyed exploring the Beautiful BC that was all around us. Every chance Anne had for time away from her teaching duties she would hop in the car and join me on a sales trip.

Some memorable trips included venturing up the Yellowhead to Tête Jaune Cache, where a bridge crosses the westerly flowing Fraser River. A lot of the way was still a one lane dirt road with wildflowers brushing the car doors as we passed. We had a wild and rollicking few days at the Williams Lake Stampede complete with characters right out of the Cariboo Gold Rush. We watched on as a retort poured liquid gold into a mold at Bralorne Gold Mine near Gold Bridge, north of Pemberton. Such wonderful memories.

Anne taught English at John Peterson High School. That meant we needed a second car because I was often away on business. We purchased a bright yellow 1968 Vauxhall Viva which she drove in Kamloops and kept when we moved to Vancouver. That car made for at least one unforgettable story. One afternoon Anne was cruising along Canada Way in Burnaby and when she went to change gears, the entire shift mechanism came off in her hand including the stick, the gear box cover, and the forks that selected the gears. It happened near the RCMP headquarters and a nice policeman refitted it for her so she could drive home.

The Corporate Ladder

In early 1969 it was time for a new company car even though my sales rep life based in Kamloops appeared to be nearing an end. By then I was a high performing senior sales rep and was spending more and more of my time on airplanes going to other cities to help someone else out. I went ahead and ordered a brand new 1969 green Ford Custom on the company tab. By slipping the dealer a couple hundred dollars on the side I got it outfitted with a big burbling 390 cubic inch engine and several other creature comforts like A/C. I managed several months enjoying that car but by summer we were moving to Vancouver and my Ford Custom would have to be left behind. The new rep who replaced me in Kamloops was more than a little impressed with his fancy new wheels. I never divulged that secret transactional upgrade.

In June 1969 we were transferred to Imperial Oil's Vancouver Head Office at 1281 West Georgia Street and I was promoted to a sales manager position for all of BC. I was 24 years old and had 14 sales reps reporting to me, rather stressful because most of my reps were older than me, some easily twice my age. I had a few tough weeks learning to hold my own amongst the feisty and crusty old timers who were not that excited about my arrival. They soon figured out that I was on my way up and that I probably would not be around this office for long. They were right, because less than a year later I was earmarked for a fast-track executive training program that would give me a lot more financial and organizational experiences.

In the performance review system that Imperial Oil used, an employee was rated A to D for potential (A for unlimited, B for one level more, C for stay where you are, and D for corrective action needed) and 1 to 5 for performance (1 for the very best, 3 average but expected, and 5 for the back door or retirement). Yes, you guessed it, I never had an annual performance review that was not A1. Toot toot.

Because all my Vancouver jobs were managerial and considered desk jobs there were no company cars, but the increasing salary nicely covered the payments on a 1968 Cougar XR7 I had fallen in love with. It was the sweetest car on the road: 335 horsepower from a high performance 390 and capable of smoking the tires in all three gears when you really "stood on it." The engine throbbed like a jack hammer as the tack swiftly redlined with each upshift. I have owned many high powered European cars since but no car has come close to the feeling of raw power and torque produced by that sweet British Racing Green beauty as we cruised along a highway. Early one morning on a long straight stretch of the Trans

Canada east of Banff, as Anne and I were driving to Manitoba, Anne woke up and asked innocently, "Aren't we going pretty fast Mitchell? Just how fast?" I looked down at the speedometer and sheepishly admitted it was 120 miles an hour. And that was only 4000 rpm. I never did ask it to go any faster.

By the spring of 1970 I was promoted to a financial analyst role for the BC region. All investments, like new service station sites for example, had to have a careful due diligence review of the risks and rewards, including a Proforma and Discounted Cash Flow to calculate the Net Present Value of the initial investment. Imperial Oil only had two computers in the entire company, one in Edmonton and one in Toronto. Computers could do the DCF math much more quickly and precisely than my assistant Hilda could on her comptometer. Therefore, every Friday morning I would gather up all my manual spreadsheets and fly off to the Edmonton municipal airport. First stop at the Imperial Oil office in Edmonton was the keypunch floor where half of the credit card slips from every service station in Canada were key punched into computer cards. The massive room contained some 500 ladies at their desks processing these little slips on to computer cards. The manager would take my files and assign the key punch task to an operator. I would go out for a coffee or lunch and come back in a couple of hours to retrieve the results.

The second stop on the floor above was a similarly massive room, this one securely closed off to everyone. Within glass walls and doors, a temperature controlled habitat housed hundreds of machines with tapes spinning away. One of the first IBM 360s in Canada, it was an impressive sight indeed. When that massive calculating device had done its work the floor manager would give me my computer printouts for all the projects I had brought over and I would catch the next flight back to Vancouver, ready to explain my findings to the Monday morning investment committee.

My promotion to 111 St Clair Avenue in Toronto came in the spring of 1971. I was assigned to the 19th floor of the Head Office and my official title was Assistant to the Petroleum Products Committee of Imperial Oil. I had many financial and analytical duties, but the best part was working directly for the President and with other senior company directors and officers. I organized the meeting agendas and took the minutes when the Petroleum Products Committee met every week in the main board room. The meetings were attended by most of the twelve Imperial Oil directors (all directors were employees, we had no outside directors at that time) and this was the forum where all serious operational decisions were made for the entire company, then Canada's biggest company.

Let's drop in on one of our meetings. The directors were ranged around a long, highly polished table with ten or more deep leather chairs along each side. The president sat at the far end and I sat at the opposite end near the entrance to an ante-chamber, where the overflow people would await an invitation. I had a console in front of me with an array of tempting buttons and switches for lights, projectors, microphones, and intercoms. In the second row behind either side of the board table were additional armchairs full of support staff who supplied the directors and presenters with backup documents or handouts. I prepared the agenda with time allocations (the agenda order was very political as it signalled whose subject was most important) and as each presentation was made, I kept exact notes of all the statements and decisions uttered, both in writing and on tape. For some items the president would ask me to introduce the subject and give a precis before I called upon the appropriate VP to argue for his project. I felt very important because that meant I got to analyze all the data and make my own recommendations too. Not all meetings were totally harmonious. After the meetings I would gather up all the pertinent materials and rush down to my office to write up the minutes. After the president had reviewed and signed them, those minutes became the undisputable record of the proceedings. At first I was a little star struck with all these very important people who were very senior to me in authority and experience. How would I ever survive this? Here is how.

After one meeting in the early days, I got a pleasant call from one of the presenters. "Might I have a quick look at your minutes, before they get published?" I thought, why not? It can't hurt. Big lesson coming up. He read them carefully, furrowed his brows and pointed to an offending section. "I didn't say that! You must change this sentence to say *this* instead." I refused on the very sound grounds that I heard him perfectly the first time. I also had an audio recording of the meeting, but I had not used it and did not really want to go there. Instantly he was furious. "Of course, you will change that sentence. I am the Senior VP of Marketing, young man, and I can have you fired within the hour." I thought very fast, although it seemed an eternity passed as my shattered career flashed before my eyes. I said, "I'll tell you what Mr. SVP, why don't we just go in and see the president, he is right through that door. If he agrees with you then I promise that the minutes will be changed." He didn't press the issue. That happened with a few more people who wished they had enough nerve or wit to say what they really wanted to in the meeting. I guess I had gained my cred. I never had to listen to a single tape. I loved that job. Very heady stuff at 27 years old.

Nevertheless, I was leading a double life, so to speak. All the time I was in Toronto fired up by my glorious Imperial Oil job, I was also scouting for entrepreneurial opportunities back in Vancouver with a friend named Bill Harvey. When Anne was at UBC, she had become good friends with a gal named Janice Rae, who was married to Bill. We four spent lots of time together over the years that I was working in Kamloops and visiting Anne in Vancouver on weekends. Bill worked for the Royal Bank, but he was unfulfilled, he wanted more from a career than just being an account manager. He wanted his own business. His enthusiasm was contagious, and our entrepreneurial spirits merged well together. Although I absolutely loved my corporate career at Imperial Oil and promotions seemed almost effortless, I also knew I would always be an employee, not an owner. I would be transferred continuously, wherever the company wanted me to work. I wanted to own my own business, to make my own decisions, to take risks and to be rewarded (or not) by those decisions, and Anne and I really wanted to live in Vancouver on a permanent basis.

Bill and I eventually decided we should start up our own business venture and after much discussion we decided it should be a marina in Vancouver. We took a classic business school approach, although neither of us had been to formal business school. I had attended a dozen or so Imperial Oil sponsored night school and on-campus courses and of course practiced the theories every day at work. We carefully listed everything to do with the Why, What, Where, When, Who, and How, and then we applied the first rule of real estate—Location, Location, Location—settling on False Creek in the very center of the city. Eventually we came up with four possible locations: three on the south side and one on the north side of the creek. When Anne and

I moved to Toronto Bill continued working for the Royal Bank in Vancouver, developing ideas and making connections on the side. I sent him money and flew out on weekends whenever I could or even during the week if I could invent an Imperial Oil business meeting that needed my involvement. In the two years Anne and I lived in Toronto, I counted some 35 return trips between Toronto and Vancouver.

While the marina project was simmering, Bill was also poking around in old abandoned waterfront buildings trying to get a plan B opportunity lined up should our Plan A marina not work out. Plan B involved waterfront real estate development. That led us to a waterfront complex on Granville Island that was owned by Monsanto Chemical. By the early 1970s, Granville Island had been all but abandoned by the industrial users who traded its old inefficient rail serviced warehouses for the new industrial parks springing up in the outlying areas, which offered bigger single-story layouts, high ceilings, better roads and truck access. The Monsanto building we had our eye on was available for sale, its four buildings comprising 40,000 square feet of renovation-needy future office, shop, and restaurant spaces. It was soon ours for a mere $18,000. We set up our office in one of the little waterfront buildings and Creekhouse Industries was born. Not long after that, Marathon Realty decided to approve our proposal for a 400 berth marina on the north shore of False Creek just west of the Cambie Bridge, so we could move ahead on that too. At the time the 12 acre parcel of land and water consisted of mudflats, railway, and industrial detritus. Our proposed False Creek Marinas would include a new-built 25,000 square foot building complex housing a major restaurant, several boat dealers, a boat repair shop, a ship's chandlery shop, and a coffee shop.

So that was the end of the open road that led me from that little farm in Regent to university, Europe, and on to the corporate world of Imperial Oil in Vancouver, Kamloops and Toronto. Another cluster of roads would open from there. It was late 1972, I plucked up my courage and went in to see the President to tell him I was leaving Imperial Oil and moving to Vancouver. I had spent many hours agonizing about how to tell him I was moving on after all the wonderful things the company had done for me. He looked at me and said, "Why don't you tell me what you are planning to do in this new business venture?" After I laid out the whole story he smiled and said, "Well you know Mitch, I should tell you that if you stayed with Imperial Oil, I would be very surprised if you did not become president of one of our Exxon companies within 10 years. That said, if I were you, I would embrace this new venture just as you are doing." He gave me a big hug and we made our farewells. In my exiting papers a few days later there was a cheque for $40,000 and a handwritten note:

> *You might want to use this money to install an Esso fuel barge in your new marina. Best of luck, Dick R.*

I did just that.

BELOW *My beloved 1967 Ford company car.*

RIGHT *Mitch as a sales representative for Imperial Oil in Kamloops BC, 1966.*

BELOW *Our beautiful British racing green 1968 Cougar XR7.*

RIGHT *Our wedding day June 10, 1967 in Deloraine MB.*

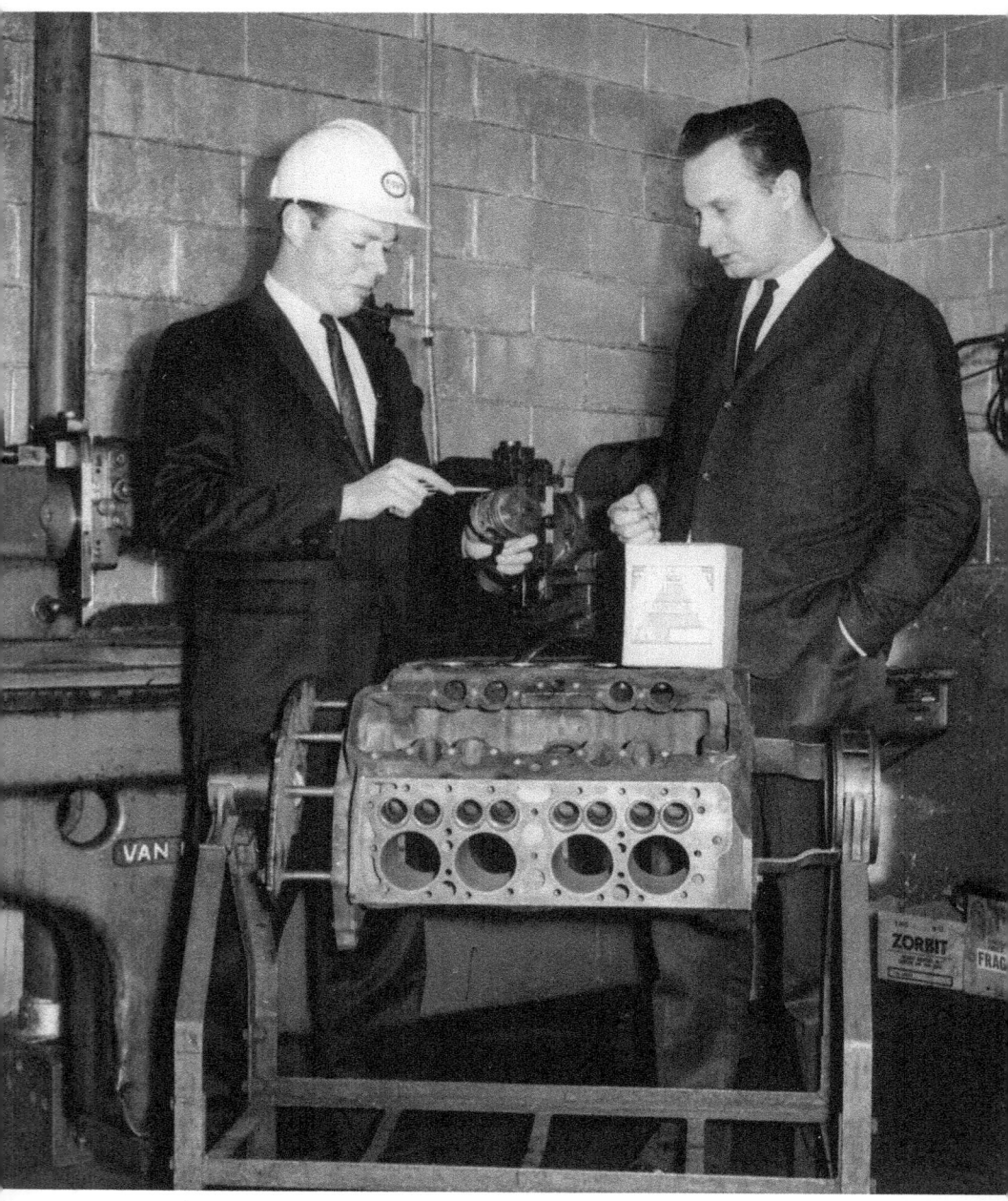

LEFT *Mitch, the lubricating oil expert, with an engine block and an attentive customer.*

BELOW *Imperial Oil sales rep Mitch by a Caterpillar tractor, visiting Peter Kiewit highway contractors.*

The great white hunter showing off his Scottish heritage with a scotch pine sporran.

Why I Don't Play Poker

In the fall of 1967, we were newly married and living in Kamloops in a highrise building at 421 Battle Street. Anne and I always had a giggle when we gave someone that address. I can confirm that if there were any battles underway on Battle Street, they certainly didn't originate in our newlywed apartment. We had a great life there. We made so many friends, mostly other newly married couples, but also lots of single people who lived nearby. In fact, a goodly number of our closest friends to this day were people we first met in that building: Carole and Clive Schindler, Anne Clemens, Gillian Woolliams, Murray and Nicole Allen, and Jim Gillis who was my pre-marriage roommate, to name just a few. We also made some close friendships with other Imperial Oil people stationed in Kamloops or in the neighbouring towns that I covered in my vast sales territory.

One such friend was Art MacDonald, a young man who was being groomed to take over the Esso bulk fuel agency in Merritt BC. We did lots of outdoor things together, like swimming and water-skiing in the summer, barbeques, hikes, and game hunting in the late fall. I loved the outdoors, especially in the BC interior. Beyond the businesses in my sales territory there were thousands of lakes, vast rolling grassland ranches, forests, raging rivers like the Fraser and the North Thompson, mountains and ski resorts, fishing and wildlife at every turn. It was a virtual paradise and we resolved to take advantage of this opportunity while we lived in Kamloops. It was pretty obvious that in this career we would not be living here for more than a few years.

This story concerns a hunting trip I took with Art one weekend in early November. Growing up on the farm, I had hunted for ducks and geese but hadn't yet tried my hand at deer hunting. From all the heroic tales I overheard at the beer parlor, it seemed that bringing down a noble "Stag at Eve," partially hidden in the shadows of a towering ponderosa pine on a lone hilltop, was the most memorable and rewarding experience a real man could have. There were also hints that becoming a successful member of the "Great White Hunters of the World" was a badge of honour in this wild west country. Being a good farm boy though my plans included having the deer cut up into roasts and stored for future dinner parties in a chest freezer I had confidently purchased for just such an event.

We jumped into Art's four by four pickup truck and drove west to Cache Creek and then north into the Cariboo, turning west at Clinton towards the mighty Fraser River. Our destination was the famous and remote Empire Valley Ranch, a massive property that stretched to the south and west of the Fraser for at least 65 miles, one of the largest ranches in BC. The ranch was currently owned by the Bryson family of Merritt who had kindly given us permission to access their backcountry and a key to open the gates of their private roads. The steep valleys and grassland ranches that we drove through from Clinton were spectacular, but then at some point we broke out of the mountains and there before us, glistening in the afternoon sun miles to the west, lay a shiny river at the bottom of an impressive valley of fields and bench lands, a valley that must have been twenty miles wide and a mile deep. So breathtaking was the view of that wide valley that my mind immediately recalled a great line in the poem "David" by Earle Birney: "valleys the moon could be rolled in." In this emotional poem Birney narrates how two boys spend a summer climbing mountains in the spectacular Rockies near Banff, taking ever riskier climbs, marvelling in their conquests and in the splendor of nature, only to have Bob's world collapse when David slips off the Finger and falls to his death.

Why I Don't Play Poker

By the time we had wound our way down to the cable powered ferry over the Fraser we had already driven 3 hours and were still less than halfway to our destination. Our lodging that night was to be a long abandoned sheepherder's cabin on the lower southern slopes of far off Blackdome Mountain. Way back in the 1860s when this ranch had first been homesteaded, it was indeed a sheep ranch, providing meat for the gold rush miners thronging up the Fraser to get to the gold mines of Barkerville. Nowadays the Empire Valley Ranch did not raise sheep, but they did have around 2000 cows munching contentedly away on this massive spread of grassland between scattered forests.

We roused the sleepy ferryman and drove our pickup onto the little vessel so that the cable could pull us across the fast-flowing river. The 850 mile long Fraser River had first been traversed from its source in the Rockies to Vancouver on the Pacific by an intrepid British explorer in 1808, none other than the eponymous Simon Fraser. Once we were safely across the Fraser, there were only gravel roads ahead. After a few miles of that there were rutted dirt roads and then just mudholes and sharp rocks that were itching to snag a passing oil pan. We bounced and jounced about for another two or three hours trying not to hit our heads on the door frame or the ceiling of the truck as we inched our way over and up the creek-side roads to the higher foothills of Blackdome Mountain. Finally, as dusk was settling over the valley below, we saw the old log cabin, now so long abandoned that it was half collapsed in on itself and definitely not a place to stay. We pitched a tent nearby and settled in for the night, but not before walking about the area in the evening light and admiring the distant multi-hued blues of the mountain tops stretching to the south and west of this silent pristine location. Yes, the boys were right, there were dozens of deer for the taking, so close and so unafraid of man that I did have to wonder about the difficulty or indeed the chivalry of actually shooting one. I think I could have lassoed one with a rope and coaxed it into the back of our pickup.

The next morning dawned gloriously warm and sunny and ever so still. As we sat with our coffee mugs by the fire, we could hear the melodious songs of birds, insects humming and an occasional animal call in the distance. We had a great morning. We wandered about and took pictures, and I made a few sketches. Art eventually had a nap stretched out on pinecones in the shade and we waited for another group of guys to join us for the big hunt next day. By good fortune, we had found a big square green army type tent, in good shape and recently used by the cowboys who rode out earlier that fall to round up the cattle from the summer feeding grounds. The tent was huge, would have held ten people easily, even had a wooden floor and door and a good-sized cooking stove with its smokestack sticking out through the wall. We left a message on the old sheepherder's cabin to help the other guys find us and set up shop in the big tent.

Our quietude was broken by the sound of a truck engine roaring down in the valley, gears grinding and rubber tires scraping over wet rocks. Soon Hughie and Tom arrived with a flourish. They had been drinking and were already loud and a bit obnoxious. You could no longer hear any birds singing as they noisily went about unloading their truck and moving into our tent. Drinking now resumed in earnest around the campfire and our steaks were soon sizzling on skewers along with tinfoil-wrapped potatoes in the coals. The many cases of beer in the back of their truck slowly drained away into the bushes. Not to be outdone, Art and I had stashed a couple bottles of dark over-proof navy rum behind the seat in our own truck; you know the 151 proof that you can put in your coffee, tee hee. The party fever improved as we ate our thick smoky steaks along with delicious buttered, sour creamed and bacon bitted, baked potatoes, washed down by more beer. The whole scenario was backdropped by the setting sun's hazy rays on the shimmering stands of pines and firs in the valley below.

Any hope of four silly boys with full stomachs and somewhat dizzy minds now getting a good night's sleep before the "big hunt" in the morning was soon dashed as Hughie announced that we were all going to play poker. "No ifs, ands or buts." We were playing poker and we were playing for real money. I protested that I didn't know how to play poker, he scoffed and said he would teach me. I did not have much money on me, only about $100; Art foolishly said he had lots and he would loan me some. I couldn't come up with any more objections so I settled down with my rum and coke, cross-legged on the plank floor, while Hughie swept away any dust or pine needles that might interfere with our game.

I learned how to play poker very quickly. There is nothing better than losing one's bet every single time to help clarify a person's intention to learn the game. Fortunately, before I lost all my money, plus what Art had loaned me, I started to catch on. I learned how to read the other guy's body language a little better, and I began to win some rounds. By this time Hughie was already the big gloating winner with a stack of coins and bills in front of him. He was loud and assertive, more than a little drunk, and I suspected that he often scooped the table slightly ahead of the dealer's approval. Art was a very good player or at least tonight he was very lucky, and he too had a growing pile of cash in front of him. Poor Tom was not doing so well; he was neither assertive nor very smart. His body language gave him away with most hands. He was the first to go while I was still hanging on by my fingertips, slightly above water. I felt sorry for him but soon I began to envy him.

The night wore on, the beer bottles and coke cans piling up at the door. When someone would go lurching out for an urgent pee there would be loud crashing and cursing as he made his way through the detritus to the nearest bush. The atmosphere in the tent was no longer a lot of fun. In fact it was no fun. Hughie must win or Hughie would pout, or he would rant and rave and accuse someone of cheating. Tempers flared but then Hughie would win a round and the game would settle down. Mostly we three were holding our own winning-wise. Tom drank a little more, got bored and soon fell asleep, snoring in his sleeping bag against a far wall.

Hughie kept drinking and he got even drunker. He was slurring his words, spilling his beer, and losing more and more money. He also got progressively angrier. His pile of cash went down while Art's went up. Art was blissfully unaware; he was having a grand time and could not help himself from needling Hughie at every big win. Hughie became apoplectic, he reached into his bag and pulled out an old western style colt 45 revolver and in between deals he would spin the chamber, which had one bullet in it, point it up and pretend to shoot. He never cocked it thank god, nor did he pull the trigger. Not yet anyway.

I had gone stone cold, also stone cold sober. Scared shitless is the correct description. My gambling world so far had been restricted to the movies, it seemed like maybe Hughie's had been too. In the movies the bad guy would throw over the table and there would be a gunfight. One gambler would shoot his opponent, pocket the money and walk out. I needed this game to end another way but every time I suggested "Last round," he would say, "Shut up and deal the cards. We are going to keep playing until I win every fucking cent." OK, I could deal with that. It was a lot easier to learn to lose at poker than it was to win.

I had soon lost all my money and was out, but poor Art was not about to let this foolish drunken schoolmate win all his money. He kept winning until Hughie decided we all should play a round of Russian roulette. Real Russian roulette. That was the final straw for me, someone was going to die here tonight before this foolishness ended and it sure as hell was not going to be me. I pinched Art's arm hard, "Just go ahead and cut the deck, all or nothing. You gotta let him win, Art." Art finally realized what was going on. He shoved his pile of money into the center, shuffled the deck, cut it twice, had me cut it too, then said, "OK Hughie, one draw, high card wins, all or nothing." Hughie drew a ten, not pleased at all, he picked up the gun and spun the shell into the chamber. He was not about to lose. I got ready to spring up and lash out, knock him off balance and seize the bloody gun.

Art drew an eight. As one we both released our strangled breath. Relief.

Hughie triumphantly counted out his winnings, put the money and the gun back in the paper shopping bag, then stuffed it into the foot of his sleeping bag. Phew, the poker game was over. We turned off the kerosene lantern and all three crawled into our sleeping bags. Curiously enough, Art's sleeping bag was now about one inch from mine, and we were both jammed up against the wall as far away from Hughie as we could get. No discussions needed, we were definitely going to stick close together this night.

The next morning was a bit otherworldly but includes no memories about the weather. Hughie and Tom got up, put on their hunting gear, drank the dregs of our 151 rum right out of the bottle and with warm bellies they picked up their rifles and went tromping off up the mountain. As soon as they had left, Art and I, without so much as a word or even a look at each other, quickly packed up our stuff, loaded the truck and headed back down the mountain towards the Big Bar Ferry. I was done with hunting and done with poker, forever.

> *And none but the sun and incurious clouds*
>   *have lingered*
> *Around the marks of that day on the ledge*
>   *of the Finger,*
> *That day, the last of my youth, on the last*
>   *of our mountains.*

4

CREEKHOUSE INDUSTRIES & GRANVILLE ISLAND

By the late 1960s the area around Vancouver's False Creek, an inlet opening into English Bay on the west and stretching to Main Street in the east, was an incredibly forlorn place to visit. A once bustling industrial area during the two world wars, its time appeared to have come and gone. The city had virtually grown up, moved away, and forgotten it. It smelled like a cesspool and looked like one too. Poor hopelessly polluted False Creek collected the storm drains from the surrounding city including unmentionable wastes from Vancouver General Hospital, oily barrel-washing waste water and, occasionally, raw acid from a boom chain operation on Granville Island—to name only a small number of the many indignities visited on that sad creek every day. On the water there were a few remaining floating squatter shacks from the logging days, derelict boats, rotting wharves and many log booms waiting to be processed at the still operating sawmill east of the old Cambie Bridge. On both shores the waterfront lands included the nearly empty CPR rail yards along the north bank, the aforementioned sawmill and a cooperage to the east side of the bridge along with the city works yard and hundreds of abandoned industrial buildings on the lands to the south. In the middle of the creek sat a very dilapidated Granville Island hosting dozens of empty buildings and a few operating industrial businesses. It was not even an island because it had been linked to the city by a rail and road isthmus.

Bill Harvey and I knew that this area held great possibilities. The city and the CPR did too but as yet they had not done much about it. The city had taken one very important step which was to hire the architectural firm of Thompson Berwick and Pratt to study the area and come up with a plan of revitalization. We were shocked to learn though that one option still under consideration was to fill in the creek to create more developable land for housing. Bill and I were excited and passionate about the idea of redeveloping this area but we were also aware it was a huge project that we could not possibly tackle alone. So, we first had to work very hard to get the "future of False Creek" on the agenda of as many city organizations as possible. We relentlessly researched what was extant on the ground, met with every possible stakeholder we could identify and find, made friends with architects and city planners, the management of the CPR and members of the Provincial and Federal governments. Our list included most if not all of our elected representatives, including city aldermen, provincial MLAs and federal MPs. We walked and drove and photographed every square foot we could access, then took a small boat and did the same from the water side. We amassed maps and charts and archival photos of the creek. We also drove down the coastal highways to Seattle, San Francisco, Los Angeles, as far as

San Diego, checking out the waterfronts and marinas, gathering ideas and information about every recent shoreline development.

We came home very well informed, knowing that we were definitely on to something really important. Vancouver was the most beautiful natural waterfront setting of them all, though clearly Vancouver needed to better utilize all its incredible waterfront assets, not just in False Creek, but everywhere in the city. We needed more places for people to gather and access the shoreline, provisions for waterfront walkways, restaurants, marinas, more parks, playgrounds, and recreation areas. The waterfront should belong to the people not just to industry or transportation; we wanted to see it acknowledged as such by the landowners and the city, dedicated forever to some form of public use. We did not get many turn downs when we proposed meetings to share our ideas, and we definitely managed to get a lot of people turned on. Like small children tugging at mother's skirt we just kept campaigning: going to public meetings, city council meetings, lunches, drinks, whatever it took to get attention for our ideas, to gather support and to plant the seeds, insisting that the time was right, now, to move forward. Don't get me wrong, all social change happens in waves and with many brains and voices working together. We managed to get on a wonderful wave, one that was destined to transform our city for the better.

When the opportunity came up to buy the old Monsanto building on Granville Island, we jumped at it. We did not have enough money to realize even one of our projects at this time—Plan A or Plan B—but we also believed that if there was a will there would be a way. The 38 acre Granville Island was owned by the Federal Government's National Harbours Board (NHB). The "island" had been created prior to World War I by driving in many rows of piles around a sand bar, dredging up the sand bottom from False Creek and dumping it behind the piles. Purchasing the Monsanto building brought with it a lease for the land from the NHB that still had eight years remaining. We accepted that limited lease with the assumption that once we got a successful operation underway at the Monsanto property, our presence would start to revitalize their moribund properties and persuade the NHB to renew the lease. That turned out to be good thinking. We have renewed that land lease many times since 1972 and still own and operate that property today.

Bill was an ideas guy, incredibly creative, persuasive, enthusiastic about the big picture, sometimes a bit scattered and not so practical. I was the operations guy, reasonably creative but more strategic, process-oriented, and a total bulldog once committed to an idea and a plan to operationalize it. To make this story short, the bulldog got to work: we bought the property, signed the lease, secured financial partners, and renovated the four buildings on the site, deciding to keep to the industrial style of the existing structures on the island. Our planned uses included a large restaurant space in the water-facing building plus enough office and shop spaces for twenty to thirty smaller tenants. We opened The Creekhouse with a grand flourish in the winter of 1972 bringing a lot of press and public awareness to Granville Island and to False Creek in general.

At the time Ron Basford was our federal member of parliament for Vancouver South. Canada was in the throes of a fairly serious recession and Ron was very interested in getting something going in his riding. His riding encompassed False Creek and his ministry included the Canada Mortgage and Housing Corporation (CMHC). Yes, you sussed it. Within a few months Granville

Island was transferred from the NHB (overseen by a minister from Newfoundland who probably didn't know that Granville Island existed) to the CMHC and the supervision of Ron Basford. It was a really smart move (wink). Soon federal infrastructure funds were flowing into the island, invested in building streets, sewers, waterlines, and ensuring proper hydro and gas supplies. Federal infrastructure funds would also foster the creation of a beautiful stone seawall and public walkway all along the south side of False Creek. More importantly for us, CMHC hired the talented team of Hodson Bakker Architects to design the redevelopment of Granville Island and the soon to be famous Granville Island Public Market was slowly taking root. With that inspired initiative one of the most successful Canadian public market projects would open in 1978.

The CMHC island management totally embraced everything we had envisioned and went on to do even more. Granville Island became a people place. Craftspeople were invited to open shops, along with restaurants, theatres, marinas, a hotel and even a brewery (a little later, you will have to be patient). They have it all. People and cars share the streets, but people rule; you can see First Nations carvers at work, musicians and performers on the corners, flowers blooming from the streetlamps, little ferries conveying pedestrians back and forth across False Creek, glassblowers and weavers inviting foot-traffic into their studios. There are no big box stores, no fast food chains or big name retail outfits. The concept is all about community, open public spaces, mixed-use buildings and eclectic tenants, even rent is collected according to the tenant's ability to pay. From 1980 to 2017 the island was also home to the Emily Carr University of Art and Design, welcoming thousands of high energy students each day.

Back in 1973, tenants were very much harder to come by. The Creekhouse was the only restored building on the island, there was no public transportation nor amenities nearby for workers, and we were renting out a grade C building in an old semi-restored warehouse still sporting its corrugated tin siding and wearing CPR red. The tenant mix we attracted included young leading edge architects, planners, artists, small businesses, and art galleries, none with any money. While not the best rent paying group a landlord might aspire to, it was great for expanding our vision of what these city spaces should be used for. When someone moved into a space, I would have them sign only a simple one page lease; if they ducked out at midnight, there was usually nothing to do but padlock their door and hope to salvage something from the equipment. Our most important anchor tenant was The Creekhouse Restaurant which opened to great acclaim: a spacious, high-ceilinged, Mediterranean lamb-on-a-spit sort of place, with several unique dining rooms clustered around a great open bar. It was on the second floor, with a polished industrial steel floor and a long wall of paned windows overlooking False Creek towards downtown. The restaurant was so successful that unfortunately the restauranteur began pre-spending his anticipated heady profits. About eighteen months later we had to padlock his door.

The somewhat louche drug scene in Vancouver was hard for a straight-laced farm boy turned businessman to accept. It was less of an irritant for my partner and most of the young men we had employed to renovate the property. We had a tiny square of lawn in our courtyard, I am sure the only green space on the island at the time. At coffee break and lunch time Bill and the boys would lounge on the grass causing clouds of disgusting smoke to waft into my office. Friday night after work was also an excuse for a big party. I would buy a few dozen beers and some vodka, and we, builders and early tenants alike, would sit around an unfinished tenant space on crates and desks, celebrating yet another week of survival. Our Polish head carpenter, Walter Kaminski, was the most enthusiastic. He would take off the vodka cap, throw it in the garbage can and proceed to drink right out of his bottle. No one went home until Walter had finished every drop.

    I mentioned the CPR red paint on the buildings. If you are having trouble visualizing CPR red then just watch any train of boxcars going by, it's the same paint today. I think they got the idea from Sweden's Falun Red which has covered most of their rural buildings since the seventeenth century. Early on in the Creekhouse construction cycle we picked that colour as part of the cottage/industrial/heritage aesthetic we were crafting to present our Creekhouse brand to the island and the city. I found two young "college painters" who professed vast spray gun expertise. We calculated the amount needed for the structures, I rented two electric spray guns, and on a Saturday morning when no one else was about I set them to work to paint our four buildings, two very large and two quite small. Something must have worried me though, because around noon I asked Anne if she wanted to drive down to the island to see how the painting was going. We arrived to find two totally CPR-red encased young men sitting on the steps looking very sheepish. They had already run out of paint without even finishing the first side. Aside from covering their own bodies—now completely encrusted in thick red paint, except for two little spots where their white eyes bulged out—they had managed to spray most of the paint into the atmosphere including, unfortunately, a fine shower of red on a long line of shiny Ocean Cement trucks lined up on the lot next door. The boys (now stripped of the honorific "painters") spent most of the next month with two buffing machines and gallons of cut polish. My good neighbour policy went all to hell and Ocean Cement never forgave me either.

After The Creekhouse Restaurant closed we needed to find someone to take over that tenancy very quickly. When one door closes another opens; soon our guardian angel just happened to appear. A very high profile seafood restaurant called The Cannery had been operating for a couple of years on an industrial site in Vancouver's Inner Harbour. The owner, Bud Kanke, had obviously figured out how to operate an incredibly successful restaurant in a very awkward industrial area, and by chance he was negotiating with me at that very time for access to our proposed restaurant site in the False Creek Marina complex (that was not yet built of course). Bud was a Chartered Accountant and a very shrewd businessman, he loved to strike deals, and loved even more to get the better of a deal whenever he could. I had just the right deal for him. I called him up and said, "Bud, you are always grinding me for a deal, but you don't want to pay market rent, do you? Well I have just the thing for you. I have a 10,000 square foot restaurant here with a padlock on the door, fully furnished and equipped and ready to go. You can have the keys tonight if you pay a couple months of back rent and sign a twenty year percentage-of-gross-revenues lease agreement." We had a deal within a day. Kanke named his new venture Mulvaney's and had the space quickly redesigned and outfitted by David Vance in a New Orleans seafood style. Mulvaney's went on to become famous as one of Vancouver's iconic restaurants, with an even more memorable bar, dance floor, and disco. They were a wonderful tenant for many years, which helped to stabilize our venture financially and to build the post-industrial culture and community of Granville Island.

As the years went by the lure of Granville Island caught on and it grew to be an incredible success story, still attracting something like 10 million visitors a year. Nearly fifty years on, The Creekhouse is not CPR-red but it is still running, with the corrugated tin facades and some of our original tenants—like the silk weaver who occupies our first site office—still in residence.

BELOW *Mitchie in his silly leather hat (believe it or not, this outfit was stylish in 1975).*

TOP RIGHT *A water view of the former Monsanto buildings on Granville Island before transformation into the Creekhouse.*

BOTTOM RIGHT *Bill Harvey and Mitch in the courtyard of the Creekhouse building before renovations.*

CREEKHOUSE INDUSTRIES & GRANVILLE ISLAND

LEFT *The front of the main Creekhouse building during reconstruction.*

BELOW *A finished Creekhouse building with graphics and signage, 1972.*

BELOW *Anne's family at the finished Creekhouse in 1972: a friend, cousin Jane Jones, sister Elizabeth, stepfather Ralph Manshreck, brother John, mother Jane, brother David and his wife Lee, with Mitch.*

RIGHT *Mitch and Bill in front of our waterfront site office at the Creekhouse.*

The first site office for False Creek Marinas, in the old City of Vancouver fireboat station, complete with a firepole and docks.

— 5 —

FALSE CREEK MARINAS

All the time we were sitting in our little one room Creekhouse Industries office on Granville Island, trying to make that business work, Bill Harvey and I were also labouring away on our original Plan A which was to build a marina. Our efforts to secure the rights to do so had narrowed to focus on four sites on False Creek: three on the south side (one on Federal Government land, two on City of Vancouver land), and one on the north side on CPR land. The CPR property was our first choice but also the most difficult and expensive. It met the location criteria perfectly: it was basically in the center of the city on the downtown shoreline. It seemed obvious to us that the CPR would eventually give their nearly abandoned railway yards to their real estate arm, Marathon Realty, to create commercial and residential development opportunities.

Our strategy was to have Marathon agree that one of the best intended uses of that large waterfront area would be to establish one or more marinas in the very calm waters of False Creek. They did agree. The second step was to convince Marathon that in the absence of a master development plan for the entire area—which would take years of planning, design, and permitting—we could do a one-off design for a marina that could easily be incorporated into an eventual master plan at a later stage. They agreed that was possible too.

Our proposed 400 boat marina required at least 10 acres of water plus 3 acres of waterfront land to accommodate the permanent building complex, plus several acres for parking behind that. Eventually the parking lot would go under high rise buildings when the whole site was redeveloped. Of course, we had layout drawings to explain our vision, accompanied by proformas to indicate how this would become a big financial success. There were dozens of Marathon Realty people involved but one above all who should be recognized: John McLernon, fortunately for us, their General Manager. He had lots of people knocking on his door with many different development proposals, as you can imagine, but John liked us and agreed to our approach and eventually that led to an approval in late 1972. Plan A and Plan B were now both in full swing.

The demand for additional moorage berths in Vancouver was very high. Word got out quickly and we were deluged with moorage requests. We started a waiting list and it soon exceeded 400. It was a great way to start a business at 100% occupancy, and an excellent way to start conversations with bankers and investors too. Our architects Sankey and Associates had already established an office in the Creekhouse, so with the Marathon go-ahead in hand, we gave them a commission to design the buildings and upland portions of the marina project. The exciting architectural challenge for Sankey's Bill McCreary was to design the two building marina complex totaling about 25,000 square feet. An important element of the design was a large wharf that connected the marina access ramps to the ground floor of both buildings: a pile-supported wood-planked structure that protruded out over the stone riprap seawall right to the water's edge. This way people on the wharf and outside our buildings would always be near the water not separated from it at low tide by a long sloping berm of rock. The wharf became a meeting place with picnic tables so the general public could visit and loiter, have a coffee or lunch and become part of our waterfront scene.

In order to accommodate a 16 foot wide seawall that would hopefully be incorporated into every new development going forward in the City of Vancouver, we designed our portion of the public passageway to be a pedestrian only wooden boardwalk that ramped up on the west side to the level of our second floor restaurant. This upper walkway also provided another spacious viewing deck for restaurant patrons and visitors on the water side of the building. The walkway circled the building and then ramped back down to the wharf level on the east side to connect with what we hoped would someday become a continuous publicly accessible path along the seawall.

We started on the endless rounds of permit issues for a property that was not yet surveyed or dredged and had no utility connections to the city. We applied for and received Federal funding to dredge the water lot to a depth of at least 10 feet. That funding also provided for the construction of a protective stone riprap seawall along the full marina shoreline. On our trips down the US west coast we had researched floating dock manufacturers and at the appropriate time we gave a design-build contract to Bellingham Marine Industries in Washington State. Concrete floats started to arrive in early April 1973 and almost as soon as they were connected to newly driven piles, we started to receive and tie up our first eager moorage customers.

The outstanding building design received all necessary permits and a very competent Halse Martin Construction immediately got to work. The poled structure was designed to house a chandlery shop, brokerage offices, and coffee shop on the main floor; a 300 seat restaurant on the second floor; and more restaurant and marina offices on the smaller third floor. An adjacent two story building housed the yacht repair facility and several more commercial offices. On 16-foot centers a forest of BC Douglas fir columns stretched up through all three floors and were capped above the roof line; it was post and beam construction taken to a fine architectural degree. Several defining skylight shafts sporting bright orange metal roofs rose up above the structures to crown an elegant waterfront building. So elegant actually, that it went on to win a Governor General's Award for Sankey Architecture in 1975.

We were in a rare old frenzy to get that marina built and to start making money. As we got operations underway we had to come up with some adhoc solutions (or "minimum viable product" in today's start-up lingo). For example, as soon as the floating docks arrived, they started to fill up with boats. However, these floating docks were sitting out in the marina basin and could not be accessed from the land. Permanent ramps could not be connected between the docks and the onshore facilities until the aforementioned wooden decks and buildings were completed. The awkward temporary solution was a wooden raft on a rope-and-pulley system much like your grandma's clothesline. It was not easy to access. The boater would park his car, load his gear into a wheelbarrow, scramble down the rock slope of the seawall to the raft, pile his gear on the raft, and pull himself over to the floating dock section. Permanent power was not yet installed either, so we rented a big noisy diesel generator running 24/7 to supply electricity to the contractors and to the boaters.

You have already read how Bud Kanke of The Cannery restaurant had been negotiating with us for the restaurant space in the marina when the deal for the Creekhouse restaurant (soon to be Mulvaney's) came about. Having Kanke established at the Creekhouse now made things easier for me at the marina site. Why you ask? Because we were also negotiating with the owners of the Dev Seafood House in the downtown Devonshire Hotel to establish a restaurant in the marina. Louis Stervinou was the Dev's General Manager. He fell in love with our marina location and our building layout while we fell in love with Louis and his maître d', Maurice Aguilar, and their delicious seafood offerings. We eventually signed a long term lease with Louis to house his French seafood restaurant which he would call "Ondine's at the Marina." With that our anchor tenants for both Plan A and Plan B were firmly in place.

No end of eager young men and women wanted to come work at this new "destination" marina, a first for the downtown area. Due to the facilities we had to offer the boating public and the brilliant location on the waterfront in the city center we had attracted a lot of attention. The marina had every modern amenity, wide concrete docks, water and power to every boat, an Esso fuel dock and even a sewage pump out station (I think it was the first one available in BC). A decision was made to own and operate both False Creek Chandlery and False Creek Yacht Services ourselves, and thus manage all three complimentary marina businesses more efficiently under the umbrella of False Creek Marinas

(FCM). We financed the project by equity, a first mortgage from Monarch Life in Winnipeg, plus a generous line of credit from the CIBC (based in part on our lucrative prepaid moorage fee reserves which amounted to about $700K that first year). The royal "we" by the way now included Bill, myself, and 10% shareholder Inshore Investments (who had invested generously in both the Creekhouse and FCM). I cannot recall the actual capital cost of the finished marina but it was approximately 3 million dollars.

Moorage was by annual contract and it was prepaid a year in advance due to a shortage of marina spaces and the fact FCM was now the premium marina in the city. That part of running a marina profitably was fairly easy to figure out. However, it wasn't quite so easy for the ship's chandlery, a seasonal retail store for boaters, or for the similarly seasonal yacht services where boats were repaired. The key to any business is good management, which was proved in spades when Alan Stovell was eventually promoted to run the Chandlery shop. Alan went on to captain his own major Canada-wide ship's chandlery wholesale distribution company called Western Marine Supplies. I rest my case. We also operated a floating marine elevator that lifted yachts out of the water for smaller jobs like cleaning, bottom painting, and propeller changes.

I must not forget to tell you that I fulfilled my promise to Imperial Oil, and we installed a floating Esso fuel dock on the end of G dock. Thank you again Dick Reid for your confidence and support.

We opened a small dockside coffee shop operation of maybe 500 square feet equipped with an outdoor serving window. I was ever so happy to convince my own dear Aunt Mary to run that shop. Called appropriately Aunt Mary's Coffee Shop, it rapidly became action central for the boaters, visitors, and our staff. Aunt Mary was a true character and a wonderful cook. The smell of her baking muffins would draw a crowd three deep at the window. I was very partial to her clam chowder and can admit that all clam chowders I have ever tasted are always judged against her gold standard. Anne and I had reconnected with Aunt Mary Ranger, my mother's sister, when we moved to Vancouver. She was our local matriarch, who helped look after our little girls and kept a low-key but still watchful eye over me too. Aunt Mary had been married to a lighthouse keeper and they had lived on many remote islands off the west coast of Vancouver Island. The lighthouses were only resupplied by sea in calm weather. Sometimes they would get cut off by bad weather for months. Aunty was a survivor and could handle herself in any situation, she brooked no nonsense. She was not going to let this kid—newly minted, highly successful in his own mind, still only 30 years old and wet behind the ears—get away with anything. At the marina she overheard many a conversation that I wish she hadn't, and never let go of a chance to haul me before the "You Are a Little Too Big For Your Boots Sonny" court. I loved her so much, a very special lady who shaped my life story and one of the many colorful characters who made False Creek Marinas a riot of stories and adventures.

BELOW *FCM site office interior: Brian Johnson, Bill Harvey and Dwain Johnson (not related). Brian and Bill get full credit for finding the original Creekhouse building. Brian created the original graphics and building designs.*

TOP RIGHT *Floating concrete docks manufactured by Bellingham Marine being installed at False Creek Marinas.*

BOTTOM RIGHT *Mitch beside a sailboat on the floating elevator which was used for short-term repairs like bottom cleaning, painting or prop changes. We rented it out in four hour periods.*

FALSE CREEK MARINAS

LEFT *The FCM post and beam main building under construction.*

BELOW *Our marina was occupied as soon as each berth could accommodate a boat.*

BELOW *Aerial view of False Creek in approximately 1983. Our marina is the property on the downtown side of False Creek to the left of the Cambie Bridge and the new BC Place Stadium.*

TOP RIGHT *Aunt Mary, my mother's younger sister, my guardian angel, proprietor of Aunt Mary's Coffee Shop at FCM.*

BOTTOM RIGHT *Front steps leading up to Ondines at the Marina. My office was on the third floor at the top of those yellow stairs on the left.*

BELOW *Mitch in Royal Vancouver Yacht Club regalia.*

RIGHT *Mitch and Anne at the annual Johann Strauss Ball where the Vancouver Symphony Orchestra played for our waltzing pleasure.*

A Fire, A Rabbit, & a Naked Lady

Scattered throughout the marina were thirty families living aboard their yachts. That was the number of residents approved by the city and by us to permanently live on their moored boats. We had agreed to provide sewage pump-out service. The "live aboards" brought a sense of community to the marina and their round-the-clock presence also enhanced our security. Because our place of work was their home, we got to witness a few personal scenes we might not normally see in a commercial marina. One winter morning quite early a fire alarm sounded on "A" dock. We could see black smoke rising above a sailboat near the far end of the dock. A staff member named Ralphie grabbed a fire extinguisher and went running down the long concrete dock to help out. When he got there he found a very agitated young lady holding a bunny rabbit in her arms, standing on the main dock a few feet away from the smoking yacht. Her boyfriend was on board frantically trying to close the hatch in a silly attempt to contain the fire. Some more important facts: the young lady was quite pretty and very cold and she was stark naked except for the rabbit.

Now Ralphie was concerned for the safety of this couple and the nearby people and property, but for some unexplained reason he decided to assist with the young lady's safety instead of helping the frantic young man put out the fire. He could have gallantly removed his coat and wrapped it around the poor dear but, no, he tried to warm her up by relieving her of the rabbit and anything else he could think of to delay the inevitable and divert her attention. It was a sight to behold. I think our gallant Ralph would have let that bloody boat burn to the waterline if another marina employee hadn't taken the extinguisher away from him and quickly put out the smoldering fire inside the companionway.

Maurice Tackles a Dasher

Maurice Aguilar was our maître d' at Ondines and he managed the restaurant when Louis wasn't there. One Sunday Maurice was watching over a nearly full house at lunch time. Two ladies in high heels and fancy summer frocks were just finishing their meal at a table near the window. They were behaving quite oddly, and Maurice decided to watch them a little more closely. A professional restaurant manager has a sixth sense when something is not quite right, his eagle eye was now on full alert. One young lady excused herself and headed for the washroom. The other waited until the waiter had gone into the kitchen, picked up her purse and walked towards the coat check at the entrance. The moment she was close to the front doors she bolted. Maurice was on to her, a Dine and Dash was in progress, his blood boiled instantly. He dropped his menus and went running after her.

Down the big wooden steps to the street flew the young lady, with maybe a fifty foot start on Maurice. He would catch her in seconds. Puffing like mad behind her as she ran across the parking lot, Maurice was totally amazed that she was getting away. Her high heel shoes went flying and the frock flapped about her legs and still she surged ahead. Self-righteous anger mixed with male hormones spurred him on like a sprinter. Maurice finally brought down the evil lady just as she was about to leap across the railway tracks and they fell together in a heap on the gravelly incline. She was a he, and he fought back valiantly, nearly besting our hero. But Maurice, now bloody and bruised (including his pride) was not about to be beaten. He strong armed the fellow and goose stepped him back to the restaurant to face the consequences of not paying for your meal at Ondines. The penalty probably involved dishwashing and learning a few useful curse words in Catalan.

Harold's Maiden Voyage

"Of course, I know how to drive a boat, I have been boating in Lake Winnipeg for years." Our cocky new employee had jumped in the workboat and was about to take it for a spin around False Creek. I doubled down on my concerns, "But I thought you said you had worked at an auto repair shop since high school?" The marina staff were standing on the main dock watching how this little test of wills might play out. On his second day in our boat repair shop, Harold had already disassembled an engine from the wrong boat.

Off he went at full throttle, skimming past the 5MPH signs on the mooring piles, creating waves and rocking the moored yachts, causing them to crash together. "Slow down you idiot!" yelled a boater, trying to be heard over the roar of the workboat as Harold accelerated away down the inlet towards English Bay. The poor man who was refueling his sailboat on the nearby fuel dock was now clutching at the rigging to avoid being thrown overboard. His was not the only protesting voice, there was a negative chorus from every occupied boat.

"He's a new hire and we haven't had a chance to teach him how to skipper a boat yet," I apologized to anyone who might care. Near apoplectic but also embarrassed that customers should witness our obviously poor management practices, I struggled to turn this situation around. The staff were snickering and making rude jokes about cowboys from the prairies. I turned to them, "OK you guys, the minute Harold returns, send him up to my office. He will be on his way home by morning." I started to walk back up the dock, attempting to mollify everyone I met.

You could see the little yellow workboat out in the bay, doing donuts and making waves, pissing off the natives. All eyes were trained on Harold, his hat had blown off but I am sure his grin was ear to ear. A crowd was gathering on our seaward facing docks as rumours spread about our new mariner gone rogue.

Then it dawned on me, this could get worse. I tensed and turned back to face the unfolding scene. Harold still had to bring the boat back to the marina and dock it. That is what he now proceeded to do. At full speed he came roaring back towards our marina. At two hundred feet out you could see the wide triumphant, see-I-told-you-I-know-how-to-handle-boats smile lighting up his face. Then it apparently dawned on Harold that it was time to apply the brakes quickly. His smile vanished as he searched fruitlessly for a brake lever beside the throttle to provide a way to do that. A boat does not have brakes. You have to first throttle it back to slow the momentum, then apply a little reverse thrust when it is time to stop all forward motion.

Harold was heading for big trouble. Those still on the dingy dock started to scramble for safety. You could now read disaster spreading over his face. We held our collective breath as he neared the dock. The bow of the boat, which by some incredible piece of luck had a flat bottom, hit the dock and bounced right up onto it, coming to a grinding halt on the concrete surface, perfectly poised with its bow overhanging one side of the dock and the stern and prop hanging out over the other. Harold was still clinging to the helm amidships and did not appear hurt.

Ever the confident young man, he was not going to be undone by some potential disaster that did not actually happen. The quick-thinking Harold straightened up, turned off the ignition key with a flourish, and stepped off the boat onto the dock as if this was standard marina practice. Then clapping his hands together in joy he called out to his audience, "What a rush! I'm really going to love working here!"

In the end, we didn't let Harold go. He was great with engines, generated a lot of laughs, and became one of the storied characters on our staff. Besides, if you crossed Harold he might just embed the entire contents of your toolbox in fiberglass or varnish your house-key permanently into the takeout counter at Aunt Mary's Coffee Shop. Both of which he did when circumstances required.

The Stakeout[1]

Reflecting off the water, the sun painted a light green wave of graphics across the walls of my office, an east facing perch on the prow of False Creek Marinas. We had been open for about two years, following many months of dredging and construction. All of the berths were occupied, the restaurant was open, and the entrepreneurial hope and dream was slowly being replaced by a dependable business. Soft breezes rustled the curtains inside the open patio doors beyond my desk. Only the gentle tinkling of boat shrouds against aluminum masts and the murmuring voices of boaters on the docks below broke the silence. I settled in my chair for a quiet morning of paperwork.

There came an imperative knock at the outer door. Without waiting for me to respond, two men entered the office. One was a stranger, accompanied by our sales guy Bob.

The stranger later introduced himself as Willy Simpson. He set two brown paper bags on the boardroom table, reached

---

[1] Names in this story have been changed for prudent reasons that will soon become apparent.

into one, took out a revolver and laid it to one side. Thankfully, for the moment, it was pointing at no one in particular. "This is to keep us all honest," he announced. He reached in again and began removing elastic-bound bundles of twenty, fifty, and hundred dollar bills, counting them out in orderly stacks of $1,000. The table, fully six by ten feet, was eventually covered with 135 tidy piles. As Mr. Simpson moved around counting out the cash it was no coincidence that he was always close to his revolver. He didn't need to take that precaution. We were frozen in our chairs.

Bob and I sat tight lipped, watching intently and quietly counting along with him. At the time it was the easiest thing to focus on. I am sure we both hoped that the fear in our eyes would not show. I clasped my hands tightly together under the table to keep them from shaking.

I had known this scene might play out one day, having recently received a surprising phone call at home one night from a policeman who introduced himself as Chief Inspector Tom Major of the RCMP. After identifying himself as a senior drug enforcement officer he came right to the point. "Our Coordinated Law Enforcement Unit has been watching a suspected drug dealer for many months. We now hear that he wants to buy a large motor yacht which is for sale in your marina. We have already taken the time to vet you thoroughly Mr. Taylor and we are confident that you can be trusted with the information I am about to give you. You must keep it strictly confidential, not telling anyone else, including your wife. We want you to assist the police in this investigation."

I was speechless. Tom continued, "Sell him the yacht. After the sale is finalized, he will ask you for the right to live aboard his boat in your marina. We want you to agree to that." Then he chuckled and added, "Willy Simpson leads a very interesting and somewhat 'alternative' lifestyle so you will have to be lenient and try to be as patient as possible. If the situation becomes too tense for you or if he is disruptive to the other marina patrons, please call me immediately on this private number."

I remember two other points from that call. He hoped a few weeks later I might also be willing to welcome a visiting sailboat into the marina with two young undercover policemen aboard and to allocate them a berth close to Simpson. Then an insight into the alternative lifestyle definition: this Simpson guy also made money from an escort business. There was an excellent chance he would invite these young ladies to visit his yacht.

Tom summed up, "Would you be willing to cooperate with the police?"

This was not an easy question to answer.

Yes, I was a responsible citizen. I did not take drugs or smoke dope. My only run in with the police would be a speeding ticket or two. And yes, I did want to support law and order in our city. But we made our living at this marina business. I was very proud of the fact we had started it from a dream only three years before, and hopeful that a long successful career lay ahead of me in this city. Heck, one day I might even want to run for mayor. I could not afford to jeopardize my business or reputation if this deal went sideways, and it certainly sounded like it could.

I also realized that my family could be at risk if things went wrong. I had Anne to think about and our little girls, both under the age of three. Moreover, during the investigation I would be in this all alone, unable to tell anyone about it, and only this one police officer to call. I made a mental tally: the risk to our personal safety, unwelcome publicity, loss of reputation, possible economic hardship, all were very unsavory results should such a story go awry or become public.

Nevertheless, at that moment something about duty stirred inside that confident thirty-year old risk-taking entrepreneur. I heard myself say, "Yes sir, you can count on me" then hung up the phone.

It had been far too quick a response. Shaken, I sat on the window seat and stared out over a dark city, my mind a whirr, my mouth dry with fear. The reality of what I had naively agreed to do gripped my body. I was nauseous, weak, exhausted like one feels after a long hard run.

The internal recriminations began. You are such an incredible idiot. What have you done now? Why would you take this huge risk at this time in such a promising career? Why would anyone with even half a brain agree to this crazy scheme at any time? You should know that the drug business does not treat police collaborators very nicely. You will be in a cement block before the summer is over. Why didn't you tell Tom you would call him back?

On the other hand, I reasoned that what I was asked to do was neither illegal nor immoral. I was collaborating with the police and might be exposed to all kinds of unsavory things in a novel encounter with the underworld, but that relationship would not change who I was as a person.

Maybe my contribution to society would turn out to be more than economic, there might be other ways to serve the community. That would be a good thing. We must stand up for what we believe. The police are serving the public interest, and they are asking for my help. If I shun this responsibility, then the Simpsons of the world will have won.

The cash transaction on the boardroom table was getting close to being done. There had been little small talk, for fear that unnecessary familiarity would only prolong the agony. We all re-counted the individual stacks of bills, each containing $1,000, now laid out in a matrix of ten stacks by thirteen stacks plus a shorter row containing only five stacks. That came to an agreed upon $135,000.

I signed the bill of sale for the yacht— scratching in the date and "Paid in Full in Cash"—gave the receipt to Mr. Simpson and a carbon copy to Bob and ushered them out the door. Carefully and with some initial difficulty due to trembling, sweaty hands working the dial on the safe, I locked the money away in our accounting office. Then I went for a long walk along the seawall.

There never was a conversation about why anyone would buy a yacht with twenty and fifty dollar bills, but I did hear later from Bob that he had asked that same question and was told that Mr. Simpson owned a candy store which collected mostly small bills. Additionally, of course, he did not trust banks nor like to pay taxes, which meant he always conducted business in cash and had a large supply of small bills. All I could do was smile.

When life is strange it often feels like fiction. Movies and songs are the only things that can make the unfathomable seem graspable or familiar. When I think back on that summer of 1976, when a seam of the unknown fissured life in our normally quiet little marina, the opening lines from the Eagles' "Hotel California" run through my mind:

> *On a dark desert highway, cool wind in my hair,*
> *Warm smell of colitas, rising up through the air…*
> *And I was thinking to myself,*
> *This could be heaven, or this could be Hell*

Had I brought this hell on myself? Maybe Jimmy Buffet said it better:

Wasted away again in Margaritaville,
Searching for my lost jigger of salt.
Some people claim that there's a woman to blame,
But I know it's my own damn fault.

The men and women on board Mr. Simpson's newly christened MV Nymph smoked, drank, and partied every single night until dawn. Each morning when I made my daily tour around the marina, I would hear ever more racy stories and, "You won't believe what happened last night" tales concerning the MV Nymph moored on G Dock.

The young men of the marina crowd were all very impressed with Simpson's taste in lady friends, especially our own yacht services guys who always found reasons to visit the MV Nymph and do chores on G Dock. On sunny days the girls tanning on the foredeck ensured a full sell out for window tables in the restaurant.

There was almost as much gossip about the two young men who were secretly watching over Simpson from their own moorage across the way. They too were keeping anything but a low profile. I recounted some of their more egregious escapades to my contact Tom but generally the Chief Inspector was unruffled: "Just leave everything alone, I am biding my time. I do not want anything getting in the way of landing my Big Fish."

The Eagles had it right, heaven was turning into hell, even for Mr. Simpson. Unbeknownst to everyone, including the RCMP's special surveillance team, the federal tax department was also watching Simpson very closely. They too were waiting for a chance to pounce on a large amount of unpaid taxes by way of seizing a very fancy motor yacht belonging to the same Big Fish.

You cannot beat death or taxes but please read on.

One morning in September I was having an early meeting with my marina manager Jim.

"Mitch, did you hear what happened last night?" "No," I replied, "Please do tell."

"Well, Willy held a big party at our restaurant and invited all his friends and all of the marina staff. There must have been one hundred people. He evidently wanted to say goodbye. It seems he had found out the Feds were closing in on him for tax evasion, so he had to leave town." Jim went on with his story, "After a huge dinner and many bottles of wine, Willy stood up and announced to everyone assembled that when we woke up this morning, he and his MV Nymph would be long gone, on their way to Mexico."

Jim was quite tickled by the story because he did not like paying taxes any more than Willy Simpson did. "Can you believe that story?" I gulped, excused myself as soon as possible and quickly phoned Tom's special number from a private office next door.

Tom was apoplectic at the grim news. The federal tax department had blindsided his own federal police department. This elaborate and expensive stakeout had all been for naught.

I found out later that the RCMP immediately put up a helicopter from the Esquimalt Military Base to apprehend the yacht as it passed through the straits of Juan de Fuca. The chopper located the fugitive vessel too late. MV Nymph had already passed beyond Canada's territorial twelve-mile limit and was cruising along sedately in international waters.

Next stop Margaritaville.

Jeans

In 1976 Vancouver was a homophobic place, as were most places if you are old enough to recall. Still, it was the least homophobic city in Canada and as a result many gay people lived here, especially in the West End.

The new Four Seasons Hotel had just opened on the corner of Georgia and Howe in the downtown core. It was in every respect a five-star luxury hotel. Its soaring upper lobby bar, appropriately named The Terrace Room, was at least five stories tall and filled with trees and flowers that flourished under the glass ceiling. In this lush tropical garden, the designers had arranged dozens of soft cozy seating nooks. Service was the brand proposition of the Four Seasons and having a drink or a meal in their Terrace Room at that time was a special and privileged experience in our little provincial city.

I had joined my friend Jim Gillis for an afternoon glass of wine. Having come directly from a test sail with a client I was wearing my yacht club blazer, jeans, and boat shoes. As usual Jim was sartorially splendid in a dashing blue suit and tie. We meshed nicely with the Four Season's five-star storied ambiance. I mention this because the hotel actually had a posted dress code in those days.

As we sipped our drinks and commented on the fortune Isy Sharp must have spent creating this wonderful environment, the hostess showed two ladies to a sofa near us. The sofa was sheltered under an exquisite flowering mock orange. The pair drew sneaking glances from the neighbouring tables: scant tops, tight jeans, one with flaming red hair and the other sporting tattoos on her arm and neck. After one or two quick drinks the ladies became quite amorous and were soon kissing. All patrons within eyesight were involved in the unfolding drama. There were a few stodgy utterances of "Tsk, tsk."

The hotel manager came by and quietly asked the couple to leave. Indignantly, the tattooed lady responded, "You have no right to kick us out of this bar. Gay and lesbian couples have as much right to be here as anyone." The manager was ready, "This has nothing to do with being gay," somewhat smugly, "It is because we have a posted hotel dress code and our rules specifically prohibit the wearing of jeans in this establishment." He hoped he had resolved the problem. He was wrong.

Now angry, the woman with the tattoos stood up and pointed at me. "Obviously jeans are allowed if you are a man wearing jeans and boat shoes? If you're going to throw us out of this joint for wearing jeans, that bloody guy is going too." Two minutes later Jim and I were sheepishly standing on the front steps of the Four Seasons.

Having never been thrown out of any place, let alone a Four Seasons Hotel, I was deeply humiliated. Mortified for this particular situation because I knew better. According to my own standards, I had been dressed informally that day. Grey wool slacks with a blue blazer was my working norm, and maybe khakis for a casual occasion, but definitely not jeans unless I was doing a repair or yard work. Had I been overconfident in adopting a "young entrepreneur about town" look?

At the time I was also embarrassed that I had put Jimmy in that position. No doubt my embarrassment was worse because Jim had a gilded pedigree, he was always impeccably dressed, and he didn't even own a pair of jeans until he was given a pair as a joke on his fortieth birthday. But now, looking back I am way more ashamed that I didn't stand up for my convictions, distracted by my own self-pity I had allowed that snooty hotel manager to treat those women so poorly and to get away with his charade about company policy and equal treatment. I should have spoken out loudly on their behalf. Our pride may have been hurt but we were only collateral damage, caught up in a homophobic ugliness that the other couple must have experienced regularly and ceaselessly in those days. Those ladies had every right to enjoy the Four Seasons, and if it had been a heterosexual couple who were kissing, I cannot imagine there would ever have been such an incident. I should have expressed my solidarity with the ladies and made an explicit point about discrimination. You live and learn.

Happily, although the reigning old straight affluent white guys still have lots of ground to give, times have changed since 1976, especially when it comes to gay pride, cultural norms, inclusiveness, and racial diversity in this city. But I must admit I sent that pair of jeans to the Good Will and I haven't worn a pair since.

Semi-abandoned CPR railcars in the railyards behind FCM.

6

THE OWL, THE ENGINEER & THE GOLDEN MOVEMENT EMPORIUM AUCTION

The mention of David Vance designing the New Orleans style Mulvaney's restaurant in the Creekhouse complex brings me to another story involving an opportunity to work with that incredibly clever fellow. David was a talented interior designer. He had designed the Old House in Courtenay, BC, the Cannery, Mulvaney's and Bridges in Vancouver, and would go on to become the chief designer of, and a shareholder in, the iconic Earls restaurant chain in Western Canada. He was unorthodox in his approach. He had to see his plans in three dimensions before he would accept the finished work; if that meant moving a wall then so be it. He often started a project by first working with the owner to determine the menu, then visualizing how the food would be prepared and served to the guests. Only then could drawings and layouts try to capture his vision for the builders. Very frustrating if you are the guy who is preparing the budget and schedule though. I will circle back to Mister Vance and his design eccentricities after a few more pages.

In the early 1970s there was an acclaimed railway-themed steakhouse restaurant chain in California that used old rail cars as dining cars, I think they were called Victoria Station. The cars were grouped around the central core which housed the kitchens, washrooms and all those necessary things. It was a cool concept and one that gave us an idea of how we could use some unusual resources at our disposal. It so happened that in the early 1970s False Creek Marinas had business connections with Marathon Realty and their parent company the CPR, which gave us a good peek inside that monster corporation.

The CPR had laid many thousands of miles of track across Canada starting in the 1880s and the Canadian government had granted the company every second section of land (a section is 640 acres) abutting each side of the rail line. As you can imagine, according to this fortuitous checkerboard pattern the CPR ended up owning a good percentage of the land under most towns and cities across the country. And, you guessed it, they made damn sure that most new towns and cities were built beside the railway line. The marina site was on one of these parcels, and on the dormant tracks of the False Creek rail yards we found no less than seven or eight executive rail cars, definitely old, unloved and unused for many years. Underneath the dust and grime of decades of wear and neglect there lay some absolute treasures. Treasures for us anyway. We bargained and cajoled our way into ownership of those old beauties and within a few months they were ours.

These were not just any old railway cars folks, these executive coaches were the business jets of the day, every bit as exotic and exclusive as a Gulfstream V. They were the reason the name Pullman (after George Pullman, the designer of the most lavish custom rail coaches) came into common usage to denote an über

THE OWL, THE ENGINEER &
THE GOLDEN MOVEMENT EMPORIUM AUCTION

level of service and elitism. The president of the railway (or anyone with enough money) would have his own car available at any time, stocked and staffed and ready to be attached to the next train to wherever Mr. Very Important Person might want to go. Most big corporations and many millionaires owned or leased these pretentious private carriages. They were paneled in every exotic wood imaginable, boasting parquet floors, deep wool carpets, soft leather chairs, and amenities designed with every conceivable convenience befitting the upper echelons of society; they were equipped with fancy kitchens, dining rooms, bedrooms, bathtubs, bars, lounges, and offices, and serviced by a full staff of hot and cold running maids (wink). Maybe not the maid part, but, I am sure you already got the picture.

With a new partner named Dwain Johnson, and a new property development company called J3 Developments, we purchased a vacant property at 80th and Scott Road in Surrey BC that had all the makings of a future restaurant site. Between economic depressions, in the late 1970s Surrey was booming again and since Dwain was already a realtor in Surrey and knew the real estate business there, we felt our timing was just right. Three or four of those beautiful executive railway cars sitting on short pieces of track on this new property were about to become the centerpiece of the Owl and the Engineer Restaurant. I am sure you are wondering, and I will not be able to tell you, but the reason for The Engineer is obvious, and where The Owl came from is anyone's guess.

We hired Herb Challier Architects to design the buildings and David Vance to design the restaurant. He suggested the concept should be a mix of old, classy, and eclectic, like the handsome old dowager cars themselves. Soon after that, David and I were on an airplane to Los Angeles, on a mission to purchase vintage furniture and fixtures to decorate our newly-built old-time restaurant. To borrow a not-yet-made-famous phrase from Saddam Hussein, this trip was to be "The Mother of All Shopping Trips." Our destination was an abandoned shopping center near Disneyland that had been taken over by an outrageous showman called John P. Wilson to stage "The World's Largest Auction of Architectural Antiques: The 9th Annual Golden Movement Emporium Auction" in early May 1979.

From every corner of the globe, but mostly from Europe, John P. Wilson had acquired some ten million dollars' worth of antiques, over 4000 pieces including windows, doors, lots of matching furniture, ceilings, entryways, entire paneled rooms, bars, pubs, fireplace mantels, lampposts...you fancy it, he had it. Everything was elaborately displayed with back-lighting, plinths, drapery, fresh flowers, and fancy ladies serving drinks and touring customers about the 125,000 square foot vacant shopping center. The entrance fee was steep—$250 to step on to the site—but once inside we were entertained in grand style, it was all Pullman. Big name LA restaurants had taco carts, fresh fruit bars, ice cream dispensers, there were fully stocked and bartended oases at every turn. One night there was a Maine lobster boil, another night a huge southern barbeque of beef, pork and chili, and on the third night the famous RJ's of Beverley Hills served us hickory smoked prime rib steaks. Being a cheese lover, I was very impressed with a food cart sporting a ten foot diameter parmesan wheel that must have weighed a ton; passersby could just take up the cleaver and whack off a sample. The door prize was nothing less than a restored 1928 Model A pickup truck. Nothing sleazy at all about John P. Wilson. And yes, I know all these treats were not free but they were already "included" in the prices.

THE OWL, THE ENGINEER &
THE GOLDEN MOVEMENT EMPORIUM AUCTION

We spent the first two days wandering around the exhibits while David ascertained their quality and visualized how he might use such and such a piece in his design for the restaurant. Quite a few of the antiques were "mostly" antique. David showed me how John P. Wilson's craftsmen had improved a few pieces to make them more presentable or ancient-seeming: where they had painted and stressed the wood or any number of other refurbishment tricks of the antique furniture world. Still there was a treasure trove of incredible stuff to drool over and wish you had more money and more rooms in your home. On the third day there was a Barrett-Jackson styled high drama auction where every item was rolled out onto the polished and floodlit central stage; each item was mounted on and displayed within its own self-enclosed theatrical set on wheels. The item might be an entire bar, completely installed and outfitted in detail, with counters, shelves, seating and lighting, brought to life with actors drinking martinis. If it was a paneled study, an ensemble was arranged with the appropriate wall treatment, furniture, and a fellow reading in his leather chair with a glass of port and a fire flickering nearby.

It was an incredible spectacle, even if you weren't bidding, and the bidding was equally exciting. We were able to purchase enough furniture and fixtures to fill a 250 seat restaurant. David and I were both ecstatic with our treasures. Our prize acquisition was an exquisite 24 foot diameter Tiffany stained glass dome, which we landed for a mere $125,000 USD after some heated bidding bested in the end by a sanguine David and his paddle. As far as I can recall it came from a mansion in Philadelphia where it had been installed originally in 1847. The dome would reside high over the bar in the Owl and the Engineer.

Now to explain David Vance's design eccentricities. We had

reached the stage in the interior construction when the Tiffany dome could be permanently affixed to the big overhead steel beams in the ceiling. It had been disassembled for shipping and then painstakingly reassembled by a Kitsilano stained glass company (the same guys who designed and built the stained glass entryway in our Marpole Avenue home in Vancouver). But it was old and fragile as well as precious and costly. For days David had been walking around the empty interior shell of the restaurant and scratching his chin as he visualized the dining experience from each of the table positions, evaluating the various sight lines towards our pièce-de-resistance: a glistening dome of brightly coloured glass fragments, back lit for effect, gloriously presiding over a busy, noisy, humming bar scene.

Eventually he determined where the dome should be and I organized the contractor to carefully lift the dome into position and attach it to a structural beam. A day or two went by and it became clear that David was not happy. "Could we please move it twenty feet to the right?" OK, that meant a two or three day period of carefully taking it down, moving and reinstalling it in the new position. Moving it cost several thousand dollars for the men, equipment, and delay. This indecision went on for maybe four more locations. I was going berserk. Finally, after the fourth move when David walked into the building the dome was installed on a moveable wheeled scaffolding. I told David he could wheel that bloody dome anywhere he wanted for the next two weeks and consider all the angles, but then on a stipulated day it was going to be welded forever to the damn ceiling beam. He was delighted, even suggesting that I should have thought of that earlier and saved a lot of money. Grrr. He took the entire two weeks to make up his mind, but then we all know in the end his complicated decision-making process eventually determined the very best location. The dome was welded to the beam and we were all friends again.

Three of the executive railcars had been converted into period dining cars so we could keep all their fancy furnishings and fixtures intact. They were arranged around the perimeter of the main building as if they were sitting at a station. In a fourth former passenger railcar, we installed the washrooms for the restaurant. The building was a big rectangular box that housed the main dining areas, the bar, kitchen and offices. The restaurant was a steak and lobster style eatery, casual but upscale like a modern-day Cactus Club or Earls. Critical success was immediate and diners from Surrey and Delta lined up down the street to get in. We all congratulated ourselves on being such clever people while the restaurant management concentrated on making money. We needed to because we had gone over budget by quite a bit on the construction and design. David proudly secured his brass plaque near the entrance, something you do not see very often in front of a restaurant, "Dave Vance Design."

For a few years the Owl and the Engineer was the talk of the town, it made some serious money for both the leasee and for us the owners, but, as some success stories are wont to experience, there were some dark clouds on the horizon. Two clouds mainly. The restauranteur who was our leasee began to celebrate his flourishing business and revel in his own scene a bit too often. Soon we were having management problems, then there were financial problems, and eventually the restauranteur defaulted on the lease and was out on the street. With our own hubris meters still in the high zone, we, the building owners, took over the operation and continued to run it ourselves. A really dumb idea: creators and developers are very seldom good operators and most assuredly they are not good restaurant operators. We stumbled along losing less money than the previous manager had but not ever getting back in the sweet spot of restaurant operation. Something had to change.

The second dark cloud was the fact that Canada was careening towards a huge recession in the early 1980s. Inflation went crazy, into the double digits, I think 13.5% in 1980, followed closely by unbelievable interest rate hikes as the central bank tried to rein in the inflation. Interest rates spiked over 20% in June of 1981. The result was that anyone with major debt went under, you couldn't borrow money at 20% and expect to ever pay it back. The housing market also cratered along with most development projects that were highly leveraged. J3 Developments was no different. Beside the restaurant, we were building a commercial office building. We owed over a million dollars of short term bridge financing that we used to construct the building before it could be leased out and before a long term fixed rate mortgage could be placed on the development. Some folks just declared bankruptcy, gave their keys to the banks and walked away. In a year or two they would have to start all over again at zero.

I couldn't possibly do that, I had way too much at stake and walking away was not an option. I hunkered down and carried on. I negotiated with the banks and the financial lenders, I negotiated with my partners, some of whom did take the option to walk away, I negotiated with potential buyers who might at least take over the restaurant and let us finish the commercial building. It was extremely stressful, he said modestly. Eventually we found a buyer, I made deals with the lenders to stop their interest clocks, and then I grimly settled up my personal bank guarantees.

Well, you win some and you lose some, and if you're lucky you get to have fun and keep growing all the way along. I thank my guardian angels heartily for the fact that False Creek Marinas was making really good money by then regardless of the recession and high interest rates, and for helping me to learn that I did not want to be a restauranteur.

I was a bit jealous of that auctioneer though.

BELOW *Railcar loaded on a truck to be transported to the restaurant site.*

RIGHT *Carpenters converting the railcar into a dining car.*

THE OWL, THE ENGINEER & THE GOLDEN MOVEMENT EMPORIUM AUCTION

THE OWL, THE ENGINEER &
THE GOLDEN MOVEMENT EMPORIUM AUCTION

LEFT *A Tiffany stained glass dome was installed over the bar.*

BELOW *The Owl and the Engineer restaurant after construction, showing cars incorporated into the main building.*

Cable Television to the Caribbean

In the aftermath of the 1981 recession, which included the financial collapse of most projects that carried bank debt, there was a general reset of business development plans in Canada, and many companies started to look offshore for new ventures. One such group, who I had met through the law firm representing our brewery (be patient a little longer), was looking to expand their cable vision business into the Caribbean islands. The concept was that we would approach a number of governments, concentrating on the Windward Islands first, namely Barbados, St. Lucia, Grenada and Martinique, and attempt to get exclusive licenses to install a cable television grid around each island. Our preliminary research showed that there were no such cable systems available anywhere on these islands. We could take advantage of the satellite system then being installed around the world, collect the signals from an available overhead satellite, and then transmit a select number of channels (from the 500 or so then available) through our cables to hotels, businesses and of course ordinary homes.

We had pretty good financial information about cable systems in Canada including the initial installation and equipment costs, operational expenses and revenue projections. Everyone was excited because the cable business in Canada had exceedingly good margins. My question was whether the revenue model for Canada, where the average per capita income in 1980 was about $27K, was even worth looking at considering the average per capita income of the Eastern Caribbean was only about $6K. To make our proforma come out in the black I think we needed to charge around $60 per month for cable fees. That was going to extract more than 10% of an islander's income. Added to that was the fact that 95% of the television sets in operation were black and white and their rabbit ears only picked up one or two local channels for maybe four to six hours per day. We were offering a vast number of full colour channels which would be available 24/7. That huge increase in home entertainment options might just cause a social conundrum, not to mention an economic one, which any island government might not be very happy about. Frustration with us might even lead to nationalization of our cable system; this was not Canada or the US you know, where free enterprise was always king.

My partners were not fazed by these arguments, they were convinced that every householder would need a new colour television which we could sell them on an installment plan, thus demand for our cable system would be intense. We would bring those island folks right out of the stone age and set them down in the 20th century with the stroke of a pen on the contract. According to that logic we would get rich in no time. My own condition before getting involved was that I would first tour the listed islands plus a few more on our B list in the Leeward Islands, at my own expense, and put together a "due diligence" report to share with them. I would meet with government officials, business owners, service providers, bankers and investors to test out our concepts on local people who were actually living there.

Off to Barbados we flew, Bob Hunt (a friend/partner and former KPMG management consultant) and I, to start our excellent adventure. As the plane landed I knew it was going to be a unique experience. The stewardess brought us a note from the pilot, informing us that Kiffin S, our first contact in Barbados, had confirmed that he would pick us up at the airport. As we descended the stairs from the Air Canada plane onto the tarmac, a black Mercedes limo pulled up beside the plane and the driver walked over to the stairs to meet Messr's Taylor and Hunt. That royal treatment was mind boggling but what came next was even better. We drove to the well-guarded wire gate surrounding the airport, Kiffin rolled down the window and said to the customs officer: "It's all right George, they're with me" and without waiting for a response, or offering our passports for inspection, we drove off into the city.

The next day we were sitting in Kiffin's palatial offices discussing our proposals. I said at one point that we really needed to set up a meeting with a high ranking government official to discuss the licensing aspects. Kiffin said, "Of course," picked up the phone and dialed. "Tom, would you have a few minutes to spare? I'd like you to meet two businessmen from Vancouver." In five minutes, the door opened and in walked the Prime Minister of Barbados. Now Barbados only had maybe 300,000 people but that was still a pretty impressive introduction to the big man about town.

I have another funny story about Kiffin. We were driving down a city street and I spied a Royal Bank on the corner. "Could we pull over please? I will run in and get some cash." I was at the counter negotiating with the teller to withdraw $1000 on my credit card. She seemed very flustered and kept dropping stuff and going off for conferences with someone in a back office. Unknown to me but obviously known to the teller, Kiffin had followed me in and was standing behind me, watching all this. After a few minutes of further fussing about he came up beside me and addressed the teller in his crisp, distinct Bajan accent: "Miriam, please just give the mon his money and we will do the papper work next week." With that Miriam sighed with relief, dropped everything, dug into her till and handed me $1000 in cash. Simple as pie, we walked out without further ado or any signatures needed. Postscript, don't worry, the RBC visa caught up to me with the next billing.

After a few days Bob and I flew to St. Lucia. We landed on a little strip traversed by a painted crosswalk with traffic lights on either side. As we zipped by the green traffic lights on our way to the terminal there was a crowd of schoolboys lined up at their red light waiting to cross the runway. Such a picture: a dozen fresh faced public school boys in matching dark blue blazers, white shirts and shorts, and striped ties. I wish I had my camera ready. At St. Lucia we met with the CIBC bank manager. I asked whether he had any loan collection problems, he smiled and said, "Well yes and no. No, in that the Canadian government gives us so much money each year as aid to St. Lucia, and we loan that money out to worthy candidates. Yes, in that we do not collect any of it back." Hmmm. Next meeting was with the head of Cable and Wireless, a British telecommunications and utility company. I asked him about collections for their services. He too smiled, "Well it is a little different here in

St. Lucia, we only collect about 85 to 90% of our billings." I was surprised. "Why don't you just cut off your service to the defaulter's house until they pay up?" He replied, "We tried that a few times, but the homeowner came out and threatened to cut off the hands of our employee. Many people here in St. Lucia feel it is their God-given right to get free telephone and free electricity and I think I should warn you that those same people will also feel entitled to free cable."

At Grenada we were in the hotel bar discussing these issues with a Toronto Dominion Bank manager. We mentioned the colour television conversion idea and suggested the bank might be interested in financing these rent-to-own deals on a monthly basis. He smiled and said, "Have you considered the problem of theft yet?" No, we had not. "Well, let me give you an example: my family has its TD supplied television stolen from our house about once a month on average. In fact, I have a standing order to ship a replacement down from Toronto once per month, just in case, along with several other household items, like the kids' bicycles, kitchen appliances, anything not bolted to the floor actually." He was serious. I was disillusioned, and a little dismayed.

We visited probably ten islands and the story did not change much. The business ethics were different, the social landscape was different, and Canadians would have no end of trouble coping. The islands were very poor and the islanders could hardly afford the lifestyle they already had. In fact, colonialism had left deep scars, poverty was rampant, and economic opportunities for locals were few (sadly, all conditions that persist today). Of course, local people would love colour televisions with an infinite selection of channels, of course they would sign-up in droves for the new services, why on earth not? But the customers would probably not be able to sustain the payments after the first few months and we would have a big collection problem to go with our problem of exploiting the less privileged and already exploited. If we thought we could go into a local home and take our television back, we would be sorely mistaken.

In my opinion the only good application for our satellite/cable service was going to be contracts from the thousands of resort hotels ringing the sandy beaches on every island in the Caribbean. Their customers were not locals, they were used to having such amenities in their hotel rooms and would obviously welcome what we were offering. Most importantly of all, these privileged guests and hotels could afford to pay the price.

I wrote up my report and went back to Vancouver to meet with the other shareholders. The timing was not good for me, by that time I had heart problems and I needed to shed some stress and some businesses. Stepping away from this venture was an easy decision to make. I didn't tell my prospective partners about my own problems quite yet, but I did tell them I was not going to get involved in any enterprise that was basically going to take advantage of poor people. To avoid any hard feelings, I distributed my shares back equally to each of the other three guys and walked away with a clear conscience. A postscript here: they eventually went ahead with the cable systems for the hotels and I think made some pretty serious money from it. I have no regrets.

The Lecky Paper warehouse on Granville Island before we bought it for the Brewery.

— 7 —

GRANVILLE ISLAND BREWING

If a person was craving a fresh beer on a hot summer day in the late 1970s and popped into a local pub for a frothy pint, the choices were pretty simple. You could have a Labatt's draft, a Molson's draft or a Carling's draft. Yup that's it, three choices, well not even three choices because no matter what brand, the three beers tasted the same, a bland pasteurized lager beer. The consolidation of the brewing industry in the postwar era had left the Canadian economy well supplied with beer, but all of it was the same. You might as well stand at the bar and order "one pint of Ubiquitous Beer please." So much for choice in this country. And for flavour and craftsmanship too.

Now let's flash overseas to have that same craving occur in say Mainz or Augsburg or Hannover. The choices would be unlimited. Every pub in every town would have four different taps each with its own distinctive beers and all of them would taste fresh and delicious. All beer in Germany is brewed to the Bavarian Purity law of 1516, which states that a brewer can only use four ingredients in making beer: malt, yeast, hops, and water. This guarantees quality and freshness without limiting variety. From there you can make infinite variations of Pilsner, Lager, Hefeweizen, Schwartzbier, etc. There are some 1300 breweries offering 5000 brands, most small and regional and therefore all the more special because every town has its own traditions and many different choices.

In England in the 1970s the small towns had rebelled against the "Tied House" control by a few of the major brewers, who had bought up most of the 20,000 pubs in the country and were forcing these local pubs to sell only their big house brands. The rebel pubs started a Campaign for Real Ale (CAMRA); they were making and selling their own small batch natural ales to great success. Choosing between a Tied House and a CAMRA pub was not very difficult, and their growing market share proved it. The dread of getting back on a plane after two weeks of driving around Germany or England, having the pleasant Air Canada hostess offer us a choice of Labatt's, Molson's or Carling's, would make anyone wonder if there was something wrong with North American tastes.

In fact, there was something lacking in North American tastes and it had to do with choice. Tastes were changing rapidly though, and rapidly for the better. The expanded horizons of well-travelled, ever more sophisticated consumers created an unprecedented demand for more upscale options in food and beverages. We were all avid to sample more imported wines, beers and cheeses, while at the same time pressuring our local retailers to provide more selection. In Vancouver, an early craft ale enthusiast named Frank Appleton penned a timely article for *Harrowsmith* magazine in the late 70s which sounded a clarion call to all beer drinkers in North

America to wake up and start demanding more variety in their everyday beer choices. We heartily agreed.

It was good timing because Bill Harvey and I were looking for a new project. The year was 1981, we had a thriving business in the marina and the Creekhouse, but we were itching for a new venture. What could we build on Granville Island that could capture some of the six or seven million people who visited there every year? Some small percentage might just be thirsty, eh? You got it, we envisioned a high quality craft brewery on the island. We would brew our own fresh unpasteurized German style lager right there, give hourly tours and offer tastes on site, open a retail store selling kegs and take-home cases, charge a nice premium for it and take on the big Canadian brewers.

This was not a completely new concept. In Chico California there was Ken Grossman making Sierra Nevada draft beer as early as 1979 and Paul Shipman was planning Redhook Ale Brewery in Seattle in 1981. There were also some BC groups looking at this potential market too. Teaming up with Frank Appleton, John Mitchell began a small CAMRA style operation in 1982 (which later grew into Horseshoe Bay Brewing), brewing vats of British style ale in the cellar for consumption upstairs in Troller's Pub; he moved on to establish Spinnakers Brewpub in Victoria in 1984 which became very successful.

Our vision was different in terms of the product, scale, and business model. We wanted to move beyond the service-oriented brewpub model—kegs brewed for in-house consumption in a single establishment—to build a substantial product company: a craft brewery that barrelled and bottled beer, built a brand, distributed a premium product to numerous bars and restaurants, and established a retail presence both on-site and in government liquor stores. We also had ambitions to produce and sell a distinctive German style beer, which required a much more complex production facility than the ale breweries then being envisioned. While ale could be made in big tubs of almost any description and served after just two weeks, German lagers were made in temperature-controlled pressurized tanks and could not be barreled and bottled for six weeks.

We imagined a scaled operation with state of the art European equipment, whose workings would be visible to the public within an architect-designed showpiece brewery. Our hope was that our on-site tasting room would become one of the exciting, creative, open-studio type spaces that people could enjoy on Granville Island. But we also imagined building a product-oriented business that would make a difference to the landscape of imbibe-able options and experiences available to people in other spaces around the city and the province.

A little background on the liquor laws of 1980 in British Columbia: you might think we were just out of prohibition. Here are some of the obvious problems that we would have to overcome to realize our vision. You could not buy beer on a Sunday unless you consumed it in a restaurant along with a food order. A brewery in BC could not sell beer to the public from the brewery itself, their own retail sales had to be through a government-licensed liquor store, nightclub, restaurant, or pub. To complicate our entry into the beer business, Ubiquitous Beer was sold in ugly stubby brown bottles, access to which was owned and monopolized by the big beer cartel boys. That oligopoly included the truck distribution system, delivery to the customers, pickup of the empty bottles plus the sorting and washing operations. Oh yes and one more challenge: the existing brewery licenses could only be granted to a company that could demonstrate their capability to deliver beer to any licensee or agency in all of big Beautiful BC, i.e. no small regional breweries welcome. We obviously had a little work ahead to encourage some attitude changes within our provincial and federal governments. Not to mention that we first had to convince Granville Island Trust that a brewery on the island was a good idea.

We reasoned correctly that to break into this tightly held beer oligopoly with a full-service craft brewery in direct competition with the big boys we had to deliver a special import style offering. It would need to be ultra-premium, meticulously crafted, all malt, fresh and unpasteurized, available in draft and in bottles, served cold in distinctive packaging either in an elegant long necked bottle or branded glass, and sold with both a marketing flair and a concerted effort to educate and convert consumers. That offering was going to cost at least 30% more than Ubiquitous Beer, even though we needed to appeal to a broad range of ordinary beer drinkers, yuppies, and aficionados alike.

First, of course, our concept had to be backed up with some solid research and development, so we got immediately to work. I must admit doing research on a craft brewery was not that onerous a task (smile). It meant months of meetings and tastings and travels including trips to California, Oregon, Washington, and also several splendid trips to Europe. Results were all thumbs up. By early 1982 we were at stage two, heavily involved in chasing permits, leases, building design and financing.

All businesses need a little luck at certain times. Our regulatory luck came in November 1980 when the federal and provincial governments announced that Vancouver was going to host Expo 86, a World's Fair. We were inviting the world to our doorstep. I recall some very interesting discussions with the provincial government regarding those liquor law problems I mentioned above. Initially we were told that although the government supported a brewery license on Granville Island, it would have to abide by all the existing liquor laws then in effect. There would be no special rules for us, which was especially punitive for a newcomer: a small start-up enterprise trying to introduce new retail and distribution models for our fresh products. I recall one meeting, sitting in a big boardroom in Victoria. I looked across the table at the minister and said, "So, Peter, when the Chancellor of Germany comes to Expo and asks to taste a Granville Island Lager on a Sunday, who is going to break the news that in BC there is no drinking allowed on Sunday unless he purchases a meal. I really do think you should be changing a few of our liquor laws long before that happens."

They did indeed change that law along with many others, bringing BC up to world class standards, allowing us to execute in full our plans for the Granville Island Brewery, and in the long run enabling much more diversity to flourish in the sector. One of our biggest coups was to acquire a retail license that allowed us to operate seven days a week. For many years we were the only retail outlet in BC that sold beer on a Sunday. We were also licensed to sell a nice selection of wines from the rapidly expanding BC estate wineries in the Okanagan Valley. At Expo 86 we secured the opportunity to sell our beer exclusively at the BC Pavilion, the German Pavilion and four other pavilions on the fairgrounds. I'm not sure if the Chancellor had a chance to taste it.

We also had to convince the provincial liquor stores to carry our novel craft product. The short shelf-life of our fresh beer with its twelve-week best-before date was a significant barrier to entry in this network of distribution depots and liquor stores dominated by giant competitors whose pasteurized product could sit unrefrigerated for months. We solved that problem by offering any retail customer in BC the right to ask for a replacement of any Granville Island beer that didn't sell before the best-before date; we sent our boys around to the stores to collect any expired cases and substitute fresh ones, free of charge. We got around the province-wide distribution problem by an agreement whereby we could select which markets we wanted to support and distribute our products into. Why? Because the big three beer distribution system was not available to us we had to do our own distribution with our own vehicles.

Another tricky law change was a federal government matter. It concerned the excise tax that the government collects on all alcohol produced in Canada. The law stated that tax had to be collected immediately after the product was made but before it was sold to the public. To make sure there was a clear tax collection break in that process, the product could not be sold in the same location as the production. We could have a retail store in the brewery only if we had someone take the beer out of the back door of the brewery, go around to the front on a public street or road and then return the goods to the store. Everyone agreed that the law had to change, but a change in the Federal Excise Tax Act would have to be approved in Ottawa by a vote in the House of Commons. Having good connections with the federal Liberal Party I managed to get support in Ottawa. I watched the CBC carefully one Budget Night in the Commons when the Minister of Finance stood up and introduced his budget, which included a small item amending the Excise Tax in our favour.

We put together a dream team of founders, friends, and associates who got shares in the company in return for helping us get this business underway: Larry Sherwood for marketing, Bob

McKecknie for engineering, Ted Richgeld a building contractor, Ian Robertson a lawyer, plus of course Bill Harvey and Mitch. I put up the initial equity (around $500K) which funded us until we had all of our ducks in order and could go to investors as the General Partner with a pitch for selling Limited Partnership units, a popular funding choice at the time.

There were so many pieces required to put this puzzle together for the first time. Under Marketing we had critical decisions to make: the choice of bottles, design of the labels, cases and kegs, brand standards in graphic design and typography, signage, colour schemes, promotional materials, advertising strategy, wearables and souvenirs for the store, uniforms for the workers, every little detail had to fit with the rest and be perfect. Under Engineering we had to determine the equipment and plant layout: the design, size and capacity of the brewhouse, fermenting tanks, aging tanks, bottling line, bottle washer, cool rooms, storage rooms, and utilities. Under the Building column we had to pick a leading architectural firm and happily Peter Busby Architects ably stepped up for that challenge; their task was to design the building with major emphasis on the store and the brewhouse, with maximum window exposure to feature the shiny new stainless steel tanks as part of our marketing and on-site experience. Then we had to contract the construction of the premises and establish relations to acquire the mostly "available only in Europe" equipment and supplies, including bottles, cases, and kegs along with great inventories of Canadian malted barley. Our barley would be sourced from Biggar Saskatchewan: "New York is Big, but This is Biggar" boasts the road sign as you approach the town. Our hops and yeast would turn out to be sourced from Germany, but I'll explain that later.

One key position was missing: the brewmaster. A wise decision was made to hire a professional brewmaster, not one of the dozens of eager home brewers who were beginning to flock around our project. We wanted to brew a German style lager, that meant a German trained Braumeister. Off to Germany we went, placing ads in several European beer magazines seeking a brewmaster who would be prepared to move to Canada on a five-year contract, bringing his know-how and recipes with him. Applications poured in from around Germany. We conducted dozens of interviews in Germany with beer being the "noun," the rather enjoyable litmus test, during and after each interview. Three short-listed candidates were chosen and invited to Vancouver with their samples for the final decision of the partners. It was all very exciting indeed.

Rainer Kallahne from Aalen, 70km east of Stuttgart, was our chosen man. Terms were agreed and soon he and his family moved to Vancouver to start a new life. Unlike North American brewers, a German Braumeister designation is a university degree in both microbiology and engineering. In order to get a five-year work visa approved by Ottawa that was one of the many professional certifications we had required.

Once we were in operation Rainer was the undisputed king of the brewery, even though he had to report to me, his decision regarding the beer, its quality, and its readiness for market was unequivocal. Later as our demand far outstripped supply we would all beg him to release a batch a day or two early. Rainer would sip from each aging tank, then nod or shake his head, if a nod "Ja" the tank was soon connected to the bottling line, or if a shake, "No, it takes a while," we just had to be patient. No amount of persuasion could change Rainer's proclamation. In the first offering Rainer made a crisp Lager, and soon after a darker maltier Bockbier and then he added seasonal beers like an amber Märzen at Easter. He procured the yeast from a University in Munich, a true heirloom yeast kept alive for centuries. Like a world-class cellist or an art handler traveling with a Rembrandt, Rainer had the yeast handled with care; it was couriered by a Lufthansa airline pilot carrying a special refrigerated suitcase in the cockpit of his airplane at appointed intervals. Our hops were imported to Rainer's specifications from his trusted sources in Bavaria.

We started construction of our $3M brewery in the fall of 1983, having raised the remaining $2.5M from a Limited Partnership offering and other financing sources. Initial capacity would be 5000 hectolitres or about 125,000 cases per year. We ordered the brewhouse equipment from a company in the UK, the bottling line and bottle washer from Germany, and the stainless steel tanks from a company in the Fraser Valley. We received our Brewer's license from the provincial government in January 1984; it was the first such brewing license (for cottage or craft brewing) to be issued.

On June 9, 1984 our six partners and eight excited staff proudly pushed open the doors of the retail store to the public. That morning we had delivered cases of Island Lager to several early morning show hosts and secured dozens of interviews. We had also primed the six liquor-license-holding restaurants on Granville Island and a pub down the creek called Stamps Landing. TV cameras and reporters, radio presenters, print journalists, thirsty locals, everyone was on site, it was a true gala event. We sold hundreds of cases of beer that day and Larry Sherwood estimated later that we received about $100,000 of free publicity. You could not buy that kind of publicity.

From that day on dear friends, Granville Island Brewery was a huge success and a little generator of change in the beverage scene. We did not know the quantum of our creation, but we did know we were in on the ground floor of something very special and we were very proud. We had set the mark and we had a lot of fun doing it. It was and still is a tribute to all the wonderful people who rallied around to make it happen, and I particularly mean our employees, our customers, a few amenable lawmakers, and the incredible support from local pubs, restaurants, and all those people who just loved our beer and kept drinking it.

There is an ironic twist to this story though, and it is this. One of the reasons that we started the brewery was that we wanted to drink something other than Ubiquitous Beer. Today Granville Island Brewery is owned by one of those big boys, yes, a multinational beverage company. Who knew? We must have been doing something right.

Sadly, GI Brew is no longer a craft operation with the likes of Rainer at the helm, and rarely does one smell the malt cooking on the way by. But we now live in a city bristling with outstanding craft breweries, and we can find and enjoy a lovingly hand-crafted crisp Pilsner or ultra-hoppy IPA almost anywhere.

BELOW *Granville Island Brewery during construction in 1983.*

RIGHT *Mitch and GIB brewmaster Rainer Kallahne in Germany on brewery business.*

OPPOSITE *Shiny new stainless steel brewing kettle in the brewhouse*

BELOW *Our new German manufactured bottling line in production.*

BELOW *Iconic 1936 Ford pickup that I purchased from my brother Tom. We converted it into a ceremonial delivery vehicle for Granville Island Brewing.*

RIGHT *Tom came to work for us after leaving Columbia Brewery in Creston BC.*

BELOW *The finished Granville Island Brewery. Opening day was June 1984.*

RIGHT *A promotional piece for Island Lager. Doesn't our beer look ever so tasty?*

BELOW *Mitch, pressed into service as poster boy in the tap room (our retail beer and wine store).*

RIGHT *I didn't make the cover of Rolling Stone but I did score this Business Mag cover. (Or in one of Lydia's lines, "You didn't make Who's Who but you're featured in What's That?")*

GRANVILLE ISLAND BREWING

Negotiations with a Telephone Company

After Bill and I decided to develop a brewery on Granville Island we looked around at various empty building sites that might suit our needs. We settled on the Lecky Paper building: a stationery and paper distribution warehouse had been operating on the property for many decades and were in the process of moving out. It was one of the very first buildings you would see when you drove on to the island, and therefore an excellent location for a craft beer store and tasting room. We bought the 55,000 square foot building from Lecky and took over their land lease, then we applied to the Granville Island Trust for permission to transform the property into Granville Island Brewery.

As soon as all the necessary approvals and permits were in hand, we began to renovate the building. An obvious obstacle was a big telephone exchange board installed in one of the front rooms; it would have to be moved because that was where we intended to put the retail store. I approached BC Tel and asked them to please make arrangements to move their exchange, we were the new owners and we did not want their equipment in our building. The VP of Engineering looked at me as if I had just arrived on the planet and sneered. "We can put our exchanges in any building we want. That telephone exchange handles all of Granville Island, we chose that building because it is the most central location, and we have no intention of moving it. Furthermore, Mister Taylor, we will continue to require access to that exchange 24 hours per day." I flippantly replied, "Well it is soon going to be the back wall of our cold beer room in the retail store, so you might want to rethink that position." A jurisdictional standoff ensued, quite a serious one actually involving many different parties and quite a lot of huffing and puffing. Eventually BC Tel offered to move the exchange within three years to another location on the island, but we would have to give them a $10,000 fee up front. It was time to think outside the box.

As our renovations proceeded, more and more materials and equipment were being moved into the building and thefts at night became worrisome. We hired night security men but their success rate was not so great because it was a huge building with lots of access points. A guard might be watching door A while a fellow with a crowbar was working on door B. I knew of a company that would put a guard dog into a building or a yard at night and come fetch it every morning. Only the handler could enter the building while

Pooch was in charge. I hired them and we put notices on all the doors to warn the innocent and our employees. A few weeks passed successfully, there were no more thefts.

One morning I arrived early at the site to find quite a commotion going on. Police cars, BC Tel trucks, Granville Island security, even the guard dog vehicle was there. What could possibly have happened? It seems that a BC Tel technician had gone into the building around midnight to do some emergency repairs on the exchange board. Evidently, Pooch had objected to this intruder's presence and had formed a wee perimeter around the exchange board and the BC Tel Man was not allowed to step over that line. Pooch was a professional: he might have growled a little and maybe even showed his teeth but he never used them. For six long hours the BC Tel Man sat on a crate and waited. I did not say patiently.

I held my smiles for later. I apologized to the poor technician and then to several levels of authority in BC Tel for what had happened. I apologized to the police and to the Granville Island security boys for taking their valuable time. And I quietly thanked the dog handler as he led Pooch off to his vehicle for a well-earned breakfast.

I waited for the letters and lawsuits and whatever else had been threatened that morning. Nothing happened. A few days later a BC Tel crew arrived and removed the exchange from our building in a few hours. Not a word was spoken, then or subsequently. It seems that the BC Tel union had made a very quick and shrewd decision. It is too bad Pooch wouldn't enjoy a Granville Island Lager, he had certainly earned one.

Mister Goold Works for Free

We never had any trouble finding people to work for us at the brewery. We had attracted a great group of talented young women and men to our little company, to work in the plant, as sales reps, in the retail store, or in the office. It is not a stretch to say they were pretty much all extroverts and everybody was a Granville Island Brewing Company sales person. Why not, it is pretty easy to get excited about fresh beer as your product. Our business had attracted a lot of press and our tasting room had attracted a lot of visitors. A "position available" poster wouldn't be up for more than an hour.

One day a young man came into my office and introduced himself as Bill Goold. "I have heard so much about you and your brewery, Mr. Taylor, I want to come and work for you." "Well, what is your profession or your work experience?" I asked. "I have worked in a restaurant in Whistler, and I love your beer. I want to be a sales representative for Granville Island Brewery." "I'm sorry but we don't have any positions available right now. You can leave your resume at the front desk and we will call you for an interview if we have an opening. It would be better if you had some experience in this area." I tried to end the interview, but he was not leaving. He asked about jobs in the plant or in the store, and with each new inquiry I said, "Sorry Bill" because by this time we were on first name basis. Finally, in desperation he said, "Mitch, I want to work here so badly that I will come to work for nothing." That was a new one for me. I scratched my chin, finding it hard to say no to that. "OK, come with me. You can put together the cardboard cases for the bottles coming off the line."

I think the office staff and I had a little wager as to how many hours this novel idea might last. I got busy doing something else and forgot all about our new no-cost employee. A few days later I saw him happily working away in the back, now surrounded by a group of new friends and definitely looking like an employee of the brewery. We put him on the payroll, but that is not the end of the story. You can tell that Bill was a persistent fellow. Well, he next persisted in bugging me daily for a job as a salesman until I finally relented. There were however some necessary steps: he had to learn the beer business (he did), he had to learn to sell (he did), he had to get some night school courses to upgrade his education (he did), he needed to attend some personal development courses (he did), and yes he eventually became a sales rep, a damn good sales rep too.

One day Bill sauntered into my office and asked me for a raise. At that time he would be making maybe $30K per year as a top sales guy. "How much do you want to make Bill?" I asked. "I want to make $200,000 per year." Picking myself off the floor, I found my voice and said, "That's going to be a little difficult. Actually Bill, the brewery is still losing money. In fact, I am still not drawing any salary at all from this company. You could never sell enough beer to make $200K a year from any brewery." Bill was not programmed to hear NO. "OK then, what do I have to do to make that kind of money?" "Well Bill, you should get into commercial real estate sales. You can make serious money once you get established in a big city like Vancouver. In fact, I can introduce you to my friend Britt Ellis who owns a commercial real estate company, he might sponsor you."

He did go to work for Britt, he did make $200,000 in a year, and he went on to make a lot more than that. At one point Bill became the highest earner for ReMax Realty in all of Canada and he maintained that distinction for many years. Persistence does pay.

We've Got Your Back Mitch

The Chartered Accountant who did my accounting at False Creek Marinas had a young son, Doug Rae, who started to come in and work as a dock boy on weekends when he was in high school. That job turned into a permanent job and when we were forced to close the marina (more on that in the next chapter) it was only natural that he would come with me to the brewery. Along the way Dougie was in a car accident and had suffered a brain injury that affected his memory. Having been a brilliant young fellow before the accident and now reduced to carrying a little note book around in his shirt pocket, where we listed his daily chores, it was very frustrating for him. Some days he would slump in my office and look totally depressed. I would give him a pep talk. "Oh, for heaven's sake Doug. You were exceptionally intelligent before the accident, and now you're struggling, understandably, and maybe you're not quite so smart as before. But just remember this. You probably still have more brains left than three quarters of our guys ever had. We need you. So buck up, get back out there, and get to work." He would cheer up and do just that.

We had constant daily problems with the neon-vested commissionaires who policed the strict three hour parking rules in effect throughout Granville Island. Our employees who drove to work and parked their vehicles nearby were totally frustrated because they had to move their cars every three hours or get towed without warning. The commissionaires would not change their stupid rules so they had become "the enemy" from the perspective of our camp. I was in the same boat, but since I arrived on site early I could claim a special spot right beside our loading bay where I parked my beloved silver 450SEL. One day I was called rather urgently to the back. There was my car, in its usual spot, but with its front end hauled up on the boom of a Buster's Towing truck, raring to depart. But it wasn't departing and the tow truck driver was fuming. Guess what? There was our brewery forklift with its forks holding up the front end of the tow truck that was holding up my car. Nobody was going anywhere. It was a standoff, and a rather amusing one for our people.

Who might be driving the forklift? None other than Dougie Ray, sporting a smile as wide as his face. Ranged around him were a furious truck driver shouting at Dougie, a furious commissionaire shouting at Dougie, and a dozen brewery workers shouting uproariously and cheering in Doug's support. The city police arrived just as I did. There was a bit of a confrontation and some jurisdictional confusion.

I explained that my car was actually in our loading bay, we could park anything we wanted there, anytime and forever, it was our property. The policeman believed me, the commissionaires backed down, and together we talked the tow truck driver into lowering my car down. He now sulked about while Dougie slowly lowered his tow truck down. Then the fist pumping crowd parted as Dougie triumphantly drove his forklift back into the brewery. Phew, a close call, and an unscriptable team-building exercise. You know, Mitch looked after Doug, and Doug looked after Mitch.

A Nightmare in DC

Waking up from that first deep oblivious sleep that follows too many drinks, I groped my way towards the bathroom. The door swung shut behind me with an unfamiliar metallic click. Oh God, something was wrong. My feet were planted on an unrecognizable thick wool carpet. A portrait of Abraham Lincoln peered down at me. I was in the walnut paneled hallway of the Hay-Adams Hotel in Washington DC. 80% asleep, 90% inebriated and 100% naked. Yup, I was starkers. Instantly sober. No urge to pee.

I was sharing the hotel suite with a young employee who had traveled with me from Vancouver, Brian. If only I could wake Brian up, all would be fine. I rang the buzzer. I knocked on the door. Again I buzzed, pounded, cursed my luck, buzzed and pounded again. Nothing. Brian had also had a few too many, and he was not going to wake up and save me.

My only hope then, was a trek to the front desk three floors down. Naked. This was my normal sleeping attire. I don't own pajamas (never have except for the one flannel set The Aunt bought for me to grace the occasion of our honeymoon, which of course, I never wore). I hoped that the rather unusual hour of 4 a.m. might allow some slim chance of making it to the lobby unnoticed. I searched the long chandelier-lit hall for any sort of cover-up, but even this elegant hotel would not oblige tonight. Abe was not in a portable form. It occurred to me that the Hay-Adams, one of the most famous and historic hotels in Washington, had witnessed many incredible escapades like this one tonight, but that thought gave me scant comfort.

Gingerly, I worked my way down the emergency exit stairway, doing my best to cover my dangly bits with my hands. The stairwell opened onto a Doric columned lobby, intricately paneled ceilings, crystal chandeliers, pink marble floors, silk Persian carpets, and yes, there it was, a reception desk. Two hundred feet across this intimidating sea of splendor sat a massive walnut counter, and standing behind it, my savior, the night clerk.

I could not walk out across that lobby. I was frozen, my mouth dry, in sheer panic.

The previous day, May 3, 1989, our government had opened its new Arthur Erickson designed Canadian Embassy at 500 Pennsylvania Avenue. By some incredible piece of luck, my little craft brewery in Vancouver had been selected to supply the beer for the grand opening party. Two weeks earlier we had shipped a full pallet of Granville Island Lager here, in the Canadian government's cross-border "diplomatic pouch." The word pouch seems a dainty misnomer for a compartment big enough to fit a pallet of beer in. Like the aunt's purse coveted by Black Adder, I imagine the diplomatic pouch "is as capacious as an elephant's scrotum, and just as difficult to get anything in or out of."

Yesterday I had arrived with a small staff to serve our beer to the well-heeled party guests at the Embassy. The grand opening was a huge success. Hundreds of tuxedoed men and elegant bejeweled ladies sipped champagne, nibbled caviar, and drank all sixty cases of our Lager. Craft beer was a rare novelty in those days. We were sure we had brought as much recognition to little Granville Island Brewery as was garnered by the famous Maison Veuve Clicquot champagne being served beside us at the party.

After the party was cleaned up our little group of brewery boys then set about celebrating our own success. Much drinking and congratulating occurred and at 2 a.m. we stumbled back to our fancy rooms at the Hay-Adams, to sleep, before the fateful bathroom search.

Crossing that lobby in a naked state was not going to happen. My panic had turned to shakes, weak knees, and goose bumps. I was not only risking certain arrest, but a trigger-happy security guard might easily think me crazed and shoot me on sight.

Back I went up the stairs. Desperate I found a room buzzer to ring and pounded on the door more urgently. Eventually Brian came to the door. He never so much as glanced at me, nor asked why I might be out in the hall, wearing nothing and ringing the bell in the middle of the night. He just opened the door, mouthed "Hi," turned, and climbed back into his bed.

Mon Ami à la Vie

Anne and I were reading on a warm sandy beach in PEI one summer, our backs against the tufts of beach grass, while our two little girls collected shells at the water's edge. A shadow crossed my legs and a warm booming voice broke the silence. "Mind if I join you? This looks like a fine spot to make new friends." Plunking down beside us, Robbie Barr began an enduring friendship that would flourish until he passed away some twenty years later.

He introduced himself by saying he wore his heart on his sleeve, and the proof of that statement was that he was recovering from a quadruple heart bypass only ten days prior. As spooky as it may seem we must have attracted each other because one year later I underwent that same operation.

In every way Robbie Barr was larger than life: only five foot six inches tall and weighing some two hundred seventy five pounds with smiles, stories, and enthusiasm to match. As a party icebreaker he often said with a grin, "I am not too fat, I am only six inches too short." His personality was outsized too, like young Kim in the eponymous Kipling novel he was "a friend to all the world," gregarious, warm, generous, and very outgoing.

When we walked into a restaurant or bar, or almost any public place, Robbie would spy yet another dear old friend and our current mission would take a break while those old friends reconnected. We were destined to become his west coast favorites. "Mitchell, we have been brothers since grade school" was how Robbie explained our relationship.

As you might have surmised already, he was an enthusiastic eater. He loved every rich dish known to the Four Seasons' chef and every Lafite Rothschild selection he ever sipped and he made it his mission to sip at every lunch and dinner. I once teased him for spilling a shrimp sauce on his tie. He laughed and said, "You know Mitchell, when I go home at night, I put my tie in the refrigerator so that it won't spoil."

One afternoon he breezed into our Vancouver home unannounced with a package of Montreal smoked meat and two bottles of fine French wine. With a wide grin he said, "I have the heart of the meal, surely you have some dark rye bread and kosher dills in this house? I'm absolutely famished."

Robbie counted judges, doctors, prime ministers and billionaires in his friendship circle, but his own calling was to roam the country looking for used machinery to fix up in his Montreal warehouse and resell somewhere else in the world. He was phenomenally successful. "I might only make a few thou on this one forklift but the second time around there might easily be a hundred forklifts in the package."

One memorable occasion when he was celebrating a new financial success, Robbie visited Anne and I bearing a substantial Inuit soapstone carving. When we protested that this gift was far too extravagant, he said, "You know Mitchell, you deserve this gift. Because of your friendship and introductions, I have just made a cool hundred thousand dollars in this city. I am going to share some of that with you." There had been yet another forestry slowdown in the BC Interior and Robbie had scooped up dozens of pieces of equipment which he immediately sold off in Brazil.

During Expo 86 Robbie was staying in the penthouse of the newly opened Metropolitan Hotel in downtown Vancouver. He invited us to visit his swanky five star room, and I drove down with Lydia, Jillian, and their dear friend Tenley MacNiel for a Sunday brunch. Robbie and I lingered with our coffees in the restaurant and got caught up while the

Mon Ami à la Vie

girls went off to explore the hotel. After a while I decided I better go looking for them. There was quite a commotion around the elevators. I heard their screams long before I got close. Yes, our three little girls were trapped in the elevator and the elevator was stuck between two floors. There had been a glitch with the new elevator's sensitivity setting, plus the imps later confided that they might have been entertaining themselves with some innocent bouncing and gravity testing. It took several hours before a repair man could be found in Maple Ridge and make it downtown to pry them out.

While the rescue operation was underway Robbie and I stood on the hotel floor closest to the stuck elevator and tried to calm the girls by talking to them through the doors. The repair took forever, and the lag time was scary, emotional and agonizing. Generally, two girls would stay calm and find humour in the situation while one would get into a wailing tizzy, then we would all take turns talking that girl down from her panic so our little group could get back to trading jokes and giggles. Then their hopeless reality would strike again, another girl would burst into tears and we would all start the calming counsel again. When the ordeal was over and we had the kids firmly in our arms the tears gushed, for all three girls plus Robbie and me. The relief was shared by most of the dozen or so concerned folks who had gathered around us. Robbie saved the day though. He immediately ordered room service for the girls, enormous heaping banana splits revealed with a flourish from under silver domes on carts rolled in magically by apologetic staff. The trauma was rapidly replaced by gratitude and newly minted tales of heroism.

My most cherished memory of that dear man involves one cold winter's night in Vancouver when we answered the doorbell to find Robbie propping up a large ornately framed nineteenth-century oil painting. It was so large we couldn't fathom how he had managed to carry it down our driveway. We now have it proudly displayed in the sky-lit stairway of our Whistler cabin; it brings a flood of stories, warm memories and happy tears every time I walk up those stairs. On the shiny brass plaque are engraved the words, "*Michel, mon ami à la vie.*"

Robbie Barr

Our happy family foursome at Puamana in Lahaina, Maui in 1982.

IT'S ONLY
A FLESH WOUND

Yes, there were times, I'm sure you knew
When I bit off more than I could chew
But through it all. When there was doubt
I ate it up and spat it out
I faced it all, and I stood tall, and did it
  my way

Paul Anka, "My Way"

When you read through the accounts of my life so far you might come to the conclusion that every day was full of sunshine and success. Well, that would be the wrong conclusion. I am indeed a very positive person but also a very honest one, so now is the time to come clean. It seems only fair in gathering the reminiscences of a self-made man to catalogue some of his frailties, uncertainties, and wounds, near mortal or otherwise. The 80s brought a flotilla of new challenges and crises, and ultimately a forceful prod to re-evaluate my priorities.

Partners

Bill Harvey and I started to come apart soon after we opened the Creekhouse and had moved our shared office across the creek to the old Vancouver Fire Boat station just to the west of the marina site. Bill's marriage broke up and he moved into the upstairs of the project office, a move that complicated our relationship more than a little. He spent more money than we had available and seemed to enjoy nightlife more than mornings, and was soon living a completely different lifestyle. Like any marriage, there are always changes and mixed emotions in a working relationship: he was a good friend and he was a font of ideas, but there were serious issues with our partnership, especially when we moved from the vision stage to development and operations. I carried on working very hard on the marina project and involved Bill less and less with the business of the day. Bill seemed to be happy with that and went off and did his own thing. Over the next few years we did get back together for several projects including the brewery, but by the time the brewery was open and operating Bill was pretty much out of my business scene for good. I bought most of his shares back and feel that he got a fair deal at the time. I can also say with feeling that we would not have pulled off any of those three projects—the Creekhouse, False Creek Marinas, or Granville Island Brewery—if we had not had each other's talents to rely upon. I am grateful for his partnership and truly wish him well, wherever he may be.

Expropriation

Remember I mentioned that Expo 86 was announced in November 1980? Well, that was incredibly good news for almost everyone in Vancouver, in BC, and even in Canada, but it was not good news for False Creek Marinas. Our beautiful little marina just happened to occupy a big chunk of the CPR lands that had been designated as the site for the fair. Expo was going to sit right on top of us, like an elephant on a bar stool. Sure enough, in a year or so I had a visit from Patrick Reid the Commissioner for Expo 86 who politely advised me that Expo was going to need our property for a three-year duration in preparation for the exposition. I was ready for him. I said that I would lease the full marina property to Expo 86 for three years (1984-86), they could do whatever they wanted with it in the interim as long as they put it back exactly as they found it, and paid me the equivalent amount of income we would be foregoing (a calculation based on the profits that I and my subtenants would make in the ensuing years, plus inflation). My financial statements were audited so that discussion would be easy. He agreed with the concept and within a few days we had a verbal agreement and the lawyers started putting together the paperwork. Easy peasy, eh?

I could not have been more wrong.

While I was boasting to my family about what a fair deal I had made with Expo—discussing what we might do for those three years when our business was suspended, it was announced that Jimmy Pattison had been appointed CEO of the Fair and would take over from Patrick Reid. One of Pattison's first acts in his new position was to pay me a personal visit. This meeting did not go well. It started pleasantly enough because I was able to tell him what I had already agreed to with Patrick Reid. He reacted very angrily. My recollection of that painful meeting is that he made clear he would make all the decisions from now on, and this prior agreement was not acceptable to him. He wanted all this property in the name of Expo. He had the authority to invoke expropriation as he saw fit and I was in no position to stipulate any terms. He was going to expropriate our property and to do so immediately. There would be no more discussion. He stormed out of the office and was gone. He went immediately to Victoria, got an expropriation ruling approved by the BC Legislature of Bill Bennett, came back and slapped the papers on my desk.

I kid you not. My world was shattered, we were done in. Everything I and everyone else had worked so hard to accomplish over all these years to reshape the downtown waterfront and make that marina a success was now wiped out with the stroke of a pen. And that was not the last of the cruel blows. We faced the loss of our livelihood and the demolition of the architecture, property, and associated businesses we had invested so much in developing. We were denied the right to repossess our property after the exposition, along with the right to restore our business or realize any associated opportunities. And we would have no agreement on compensation until we had gone to an Arbitration court. They offered an absurdly low bid which I rejected out of hand and the fight of my life was on.

To jump ahead a bit in this story for a moment, our case was not heard until after the fair closed, and we were forced to fight out a long, complicated, and incredibly mean-spirited hearing. Mean-spirited because part of the opening statement by their lawyer on behalf of the BC government declared that the property really had little value; that the future business was worthless because Mitch Taylor was the key to its success; he had a serious heart issue (more on that later) and was therefore unlikely to live.

We persevered. We oversaw the eviction of the tenants and live aboards, the moving of our boats to other locations, and watched as the marina was demolished for Expo 86 to be built on the site. The fair could have functioned beautifully with a marina on its grounds. Or the post-fair plan could have provided some opportunities for existing businesses to return or for local stakeholders and residents to plant new seeds on the shores of False Creek. But it didn't. Ultimately the BC Government decided that after the fair the entire site— some 220 acres of downtown Vancouver waterfront— should be packaged as a single property and sold to a foreign investor, Lee Ka Shing of Hong Kong. None of the original lease holders and local businesses had a chance to return to their interests in False Creek.

We did eventually go to court and we received a fair settlement from the arbitrator (more than double the original low-ball offer) although as anyone who has been through an arbitration well knows, both parties come away from a successful arbitration with only half of their baby. We were granted some compensation for the existing lease, but we missed out on any potential value for the future of the business and the property development, which would be an enormous valuation. I estimate that our little 12 acre property, given what happened to real estate in Vancouver and to that downtown waterfront site, would be worth a very sizeable fortune today. (I console my girls of this loss by explaining that they would be insufferable characters if they had grown up with that kind of wealth and privilege).

Expo 86 was a huge success, as everyone knows, but for us it was a great loss, our business, lifestyle, and future plans had been snuffed out capriciously. And it could easily have gone another way.

My credo emphasizes facing each new day with no regrets and no grudges. Nonetheless, I still refuse to buy groceries at Save on Foods.

Heart

My entrepreneurial life had always been stressful, every day was filled with challenges that sometimes seemed insurmountable as you can tell from what you have read so far. I worked incessantly and used to joke to Anne that I was going to "burn the candles at both ends, sprint hard and die before I'm 40." Such was my passion to succeed, to pull myself up out of the survival mode of my youth.

The best stress relief is always exercise, so each morning I went downtown to the YMCA for an exercise class and to join some buddies for a run around Stanley Park. Early in 1982 I started to notice that my running times were lagging and, being a bit competitive, I pushed myself even harder. It did not get better. I went to my doctor, who said, "You are just stressed. There is nothing wrong with you, you are only 37 years old. Go spend a week in Palm Springs and relax." I did just that, but I noticed that when I went for a morning run in the hot weather there, I got pains in my right arm after a few minutes running. Weeks later I went on a business trip to Golden Colorado to get some brewery advice from the Coors Brewery people. I checked into a small hotel and was given a room on the third floor. Carrying my suitcase up the three floors was very hard work and the pain in my right arm came back. I figured the 6,000 foot altitude must have been affecting me. They had a beautiful composite running track but when I tried it out the next morning, I could hardly run at all. Something was very wrong. I was sure then that I had a heart problem regardless of what my GP thought.

Back in Vancouver I pushed my doctor for a heart stress test at UBC. I was not on the treadmill machine for more than a minute when a bright young cardiologist named Dr. Vicki Bernstein came into the room, took one look at the heart monitors and said, "Stop that machine. Lay down on the gurney there, don't move for five minutes and then come see me in my office." Now sitting across the desk from her she declared, "You have a serious problem young man. I am sure you have atherosclerosis, that means some of your heart arteries are severely restricted or maybe even blocked by plaque. Your arteries are starving for blood when your body demands it, like when running hard or at high altitudes. That creates angina pain. It can telegraph into the arm, as it does in your case. You will undoubtedly end up with a serious heart attack if we cannot get bypass surgery in time. We need to get you an angiogram to confirm this diagnosis. I will order that right away." This was December 1982 and I was 38 years old. Open-heart bypass surgery was a relatively new procedure, and the waiting list was four to six months. I was a bit cavalier with her. I said, "Well that's fine but I do hope this process will not interfere with our family Christmas trip to Maui, which is scheduled for next Friday." She took off her glasses, leaned across the desk and said in a stern voice, "Mister Taylor, if you do not take this problem seriously, you will not be going to Hawaii, you will be dead." I burst into tears. She had made her point.

We did go to Maui, I did take it easy and by March 1983, I was undergoing a quadruple bypass in Vancouver General Hospital. Thank god the operation was a success and most of the arterial workarounds stitched together with a vein from my leg have lasted to this day, as has my relationship with the wonderful Dr. Bernstein. She tells me that I am not only her oldest surviving bypass operation but her sweetest patient. Smile.

The heart surgery and ensuing months-long recovery period were incredibly hard on everyone involved, especially Anne and the girls. Lydia was ten and Jillian was nine; they did not enjoy watching the informative PBS documentary showing open-heart surgery nor visiting me in the hospital and seeing all those tubes sticking out of me. I had nearly died which is enough stress to put on a family, but so had my business career. I knew I had to make a complete change in my lifestyle and my workload. I had no less than thirteen businesses[1] that I was involved in, some of them start-ups, but all of them requiring my direct involvement. These had ballooned out of my determination to succeed and grow fast, but also my inability to say no. Now my body had said no, and it was time for my actions to follow suit. I went to work to extricate myself from those companies. In some cases, I gave my shares away to my partners, or transferred management to others, or just walked away. I decided to concentrate on the three businesses that still needed my attention: Creekhouse, the soon-to-be-expropriated marina, and the not-yet-open brewery.

---

[1] Taylor/Harvey Industries, Creekhouse Industries, False Creek Marinas, False Creek Chandlery, False Creek Yacht Services, TackMar Distributors (chandlery products), J3 Developments (land-development in Surrey), Owl and the Engineer Restaurant, Chancellors Racket Club, Intercable Communications, Master Mariners (California-based sailboat building company), Black Gavin Insurance, Granville Island Brewery.

Separation

I was discombobulated. I saw myself as having failed personally and professionally. I had burned out at 38 years old and felt that everything had gone wrong. I blamed myself and was too proud to seek counselling. A perfect storm was brewing inside my head and I saw no way out. Within months our marriage was a mess and Anne and I had split up. I was living alone in a two-bedroom apartment on Birch Street. It was rock bottom: no wife, no family, no marina, a bad heart, a bachelor apartment, and it was all my fault. What an unacceptably terrible price to pay for all of that entrepreneurial full-speed-ahead determination. I had spent my life so totally committed to my career and the businesses I was creating. I never questioned the reality that Anne was the parent left at home with the kids while I went off to work for long hours every day. It had been a totally unbalanced work/life situation and an unbalanced partnership, and I felt that I had failed all three of them. I began to see that as I sat alone in my apartment trying to figure out what had gone so terribly wrong.

I had lost touch with that seven-year old boy sitting on the train west of Winnipeg and how he had promised to live his life. How could I get back to that place of optimism and openness? I realized I had closed off my emotions in order to survive, beginning with the emotional turmoil of leaving my family at such a young age to create a new life for myself with the Browns. I had hardened that protective shell in my drive for success and perpetual forward motion. That shell now needed to crack so that I could put aside ambition, be compassionate with myself, and become wholly available to my family. I no longer needed protection. I needed to take stock and to grow.

My first decision was that only I could build my relationships with Lydia and Jillian. Anne and I might not get back together again for lots of reasons, but I could not allow my children to drift away from me as is the unfortunate result in so many family breakups. My connection with my girls had to come first, before any business or other measure of happiness or achievement. From that day on they became my number one priority. A reset was overdue, and this was the best place to start in acknowledging what was important. I began to take an active part in their lives. I had them over whenever I could and made more time to just be present with them. I learned how to cook, building up from the low entry start of beer chicken and boiled broccoli with Kraft parmesan. Anne and I shared their parenting like never before.

The second decision came a few months later, as I watched Anne bravely rebuilding her life. In doing so she started to take some incredibly effective personal development courses and to excel in her own projects. Eventually (and I do mean eventually because I was really stuck in my pit of despair) she generously shared her results and convinced me that some "inner-work" courses might do me a lot of good too. The program was called the Pursuit of Excellence, a series of week-long classes over several months. Participants would learn what drives them to do things, what stops them from achieving things, and how to alter that context. The challenge was not to feel trapped by others or by circumstances or the old unexamined scripts you allowed to define you, but instead to change your own attitudes. A "light bulb course" I came to call it. People would be telling their stories and as I sat there a light bulb would go on in my head, "My god man, that is exactly what is happening to me, no wonder such and such did not result."

It may come as no surprise that I had not previously had any training or experience in making a study of my own psyche or cultivating emotional intelligence. Thus, the Pursuit courses were timely and foundational for my personal growth. It wasn't easy to open myself to that kind of vulnerability and self-reflection, but I think the group setting made it easier to trust the process and invite some truths or transformations I might otherwise avoid. It also helped to connect with and support other people who were positive and to move away from sources of negative energy or judgement. I now had a few more tools and could acknowledge some elements I was missing or neglecting. I knew I needed to take a renewed inventory of the things I was most grateful for and intentionally pursue the things I value in my life. Of course, Anne was at the top of that list. Going forward I would look after my health and my family first, and my business interests and world-building projects could come after that. I am pretty good at commitment once I can see my choices clearly. To paraphrase my hero Winston Churchill "I was able to climb out of my stygian gloom and take back control of my destiny."

After a life of hardscrabble headlong sprinting, I came to the realization that I didn't need to run anymore, nor prove anything to anyone, especially myself. I already had everything that mattered. I learned to love myself and all those around me. The best possible outcome was that Anne and I rebuilt our relationship on an even stronger footing. We saw what we had originally loved in each other and after eighteen months of separation we put our marriage and our lives back together.

The 1980s had brought more Monty Python "flesh wounds" than I had bargained for. It was a rough decade that brought me to a welcome reset, a reminder that I was not some kind of superhero.

I was in fact mortal and I had come very close to proving it. I had, however, been given a second chance to rebuild a life that was a bit more balanced and reflective. I never lost my appetite to take on Sisyphean tasks. But thankfully, once I had learned to consult the village and to take off my armour regularly, I was able to plan the ascents more clearly.

PREVIOUS PAGE *Our even happier "Second Wedding" family foursome in 1985.*

BELOW *Anne and I enjoying a picnic lunch in the French countryside.*

TOP RIGHT *Sketch of my potential château/Relais, tee hee.*

BOTTOM RIGHT *Endless rounds of Roquefort cheeses in their massive caves.*

IT'S ONLY A FLESH WOUND

Inspector Clouseau Visits Sarlat-la-Canéda

To cement our renewed commitment to each other, Anne and I embarked on a six week second honeymoon in the summer of 1985. Anne's mom looked after the girls, and we had a resplendent time driving around France.

As we started up a steep incline our little Renault 12 groaned under the weight of our recent acquisitions: sweet noble-rot-infected Sauternes, Monbazillacs, and full bodied reds with such famous names as Saint-Émilion, Margaux, Haut-Brion, and Pauillac. Four cases in that little trunk. Not sure what on earth we were thinking when we bought all that wine. It was going to be difficult getting through Canadian Customs on the way home. Unless we drank it all. That was not all Anne and I had stuffed in the *coffre* of our little Renault. There were big rounds of smelly Roquefort cheese, delicious dry sausages, tinned *pâté de foie gras*, crackers, cookies and sweets. Surely it was enough food and wine to last for at least twenty more picnics complimented by fresh baguettes and tomatoes that we would buy each midday.

Our baby grand tour of France had swung us west and south from the Loire, down the Atlantic coast to Bordeaux, east along the Dordogne, visiting vineyards and châteaux at every opportunity. We were now climbing up a winding two lane highway through some fractured limestone foothills marking the edge of the great French Central Massif.

One of our favourite areas was along the Garonne River southeast of Bordeaux near Graves where the sauterne châteaux and vineyards are located. Sauterne is a very sweet dessert wine with a distinguished taste caused by a beneficial infection of the vines with a grey fungus called botrytis cinera or "noble rot". The wine is rare and expensive, because the grapes need to be left on the vines as late as possible each autumn and picked over several times. Indeed, a bottle of one of the most famous sauternes, Château Yquem, sells for more than $1000, although we found lots of great tasting alternatives for a lot less than that in 1985.

This area of Sauternes was the perfect setting for one of my entrepreneurial dreams. I had been formulating a concept that one day we would acquire a small 10 or 12 room Relais or château and now finally the location was obvious. The ultimate location was right here in Barsac just back from the slow moving Garonne River, surrounded by 20 acres of

Semillon, Muscadelle and Sauvignon Blanc vineyards on gently sloping hills, dotted with shady copses of sycamore trees. But that is just the setting, just the beginning of the dream, there is more you must know. Anne and I were going to operate a special destination hotel; it is best to explain it from a client perspective.

Each year we would publish a catalogue with the CVs of two dozen interesting people who would be our featured guests in the Relais for one or two weeks that season. The list of guests would be as eclectic as our interests and hopefully that would grow and expand over time: artists, authors, musicians, intellectuals, philosophers, wine makers, chefs, walkers, talkers and perhaps even the odd cynical mocker to keep the debates going. As a prospective client you would read the catalogue, see someone you were interested in meeting—say an emerging author or painter—and then book a week-long stay with us to coincide with the desired thinker-in-residence.

During that stay you could join the featured author for outdoor writing classes under the plane trees or set up an easel beside an esteemed painter in a nearby village. There would be lavish Monet picnics and decadent meals followed by intoxicating and challenging after-dinner conversations

Inspector Clouseau Visits Sarlat-la-Canéda

(à la Bloomsbury Circle) and musical performances. We could arrange trips to the Gouffre de Padirac caves with a spelunking expert or visits to the great abbeys and cathedrals along the ancient pilgrimage routes that traverse the region. Or guests could help with the wine harvest under the tutelage of some famous winemaker. Whatever you can imagine you would like to do on a trip to the Dordogne, we could arrange it. Yes, you would have to pay handsomely for this privileged opportunity, but the uniqueness of the experience would be so rewarding you would book your special room and guests for ten years in advance. Might I take your deposit now, ma'am?

Before I leave this subject, I must add that Anne was a bit skeptical when I laid out this grand concept. She thought for a moment then frowned across the center console, "Sure Mitch, I think this is a great idea but I am not nearly so excited as you are. I keep getting this image of the spirited after dinner conversations going on in the parlour below, you holding forth with all our guests, refilling glasses of sauternes and cognacs, and guess what? I see myself upstairs in a guestroom, madly changing the sheets. I don't like that image one little bit." *Post Script: we never did buy a hotel so that image didn't get tested.*

We spent a few days touring in the Perigord–Limousin region, visiting Lascaux's 17,000 year old cave paintings and The National Museum of Prehistory in Les Eyzies de Tayac (oh I loved to say that name). We were on our way to Sarlat-la-Canéda, a medieval town dating from the 8th century, just 10km further on. We did not have a hotel reservation as was our wont that trip; we took our chances wherever we decided to stop for the night. If the modestly priced hotels were scarce we would just ask at more upscale hotels until someone had an opening at some price. Such was the case on a hot August afternoon in tourist heavy Sarlat. After being turned away—enduring the condescending "non"s of several innkeepers—we eventually knocked on the massive oak doors of an imposing château hotel located on a promontory overlooking the walls of the ancient town.

Although the year was 1985, I was still very much in love with Peter Sellers and his silly performances in the *Pink Panther* movies. I had been practicing his ridiculous faux French accent relentlessly on my poor wife as we drove along in the car; by now my nearly perfect "Chief Inspector Clouseau" impression was as warped and unintelligible as Peter Sellers'. Crunching stones on the gravel drive, our little Renault came to a halt near the front steps of the château. I jumped out and without breaking stride I swung open the heavy door, marched up to the front desk and stood expectantly in front of the distinguished older lady seated there. She was knitting like Madame LaFarge and did not even look up until I had cleared my throat a couple of times. "Yes, what can I do for you today?" Ever confident still, Chief Inspector Clouseau said, "Goood Evenink Madaam, Doo you have a rheum?" The lady put down her knitting and looked at me searchingly for a few moments. She then picked up the needles and started knitting again. After a long pause she said very firmly and dismissively, as only a Gallic person can, in a strong French accent "Non." I was obviously not doing well. I didn't know how to segue into a normal accent or a serious follow-up question, and I had no hope she would see the humour in the situation, so I stood there helplessly.

On the other side of the lobby two wide glass-paned doors led into the dining room. At a table near the doors a young man was working on a big stack of papers. He had overheard this conversation and you could see he was smiling and probably enjoying the scene. He put down his pen, looked up at me and said in perfect English, "Where the hell are you from?" I stammered my apologies to the lady and told him that we were Canadian tourists looking to rent a room for a few nights. He thought about that for a moment then got up and came over to the desk. "Mother, please give this gentleman a room, he is a Canadian and he was only being silly with his Inspector Clouseau accent, which, by the way sir, is not very good." With that the tension eased, we got the most magnificent room with floor to ceiling windows overlooking the terrace, the broad manicured château gardens and the town below. It was a bit expensive, but I put that down to a price I should have paid to get a few more French lessons. The son had just returned to Sarlat from studying in the US. Fortunately for me, he shared my enthusiasm for and delight in the silly Inspector.

The Chief Inspector accompanied us during our remaining weeks in southern France but I didn't avail myself of his assistance with any more hotel reservations. We only spent a few days in Sarlat because its picture perfect medieval town had attracted hordes of other tourists. It was also being used as a film set so we didn't even get to explore the historic Saint Sacerdos cathedral which dates from an original Benedictine Abbey founded in 1091.

The remaining days of our trip took us slowly along the Mediterranean coast as far as Monte Carlo before turning north to sip some of the fabulous wines of the Côtes de Rhône on our way back to Paris to return the car and head home. We had whittled our supply of wine down to an arm-stretching 15 bottles by the time we boarded the plane in Amsterdam for Vancouver. Due to the fact I was in the restaurant business a kindly customs officer waived us through with our wines, rounds of cheese, canned pâtés and air-dried sausages. I was very tempted to have the Chief Inspector thank the kind officer, but Anne wisely gave me "the look" and we walked suavely and untaxed out of Canada Customs.

Lydia and Jillian circa 1977.

— 9 —

WORDS OF ADVICE

When I think of the audience for this book, it is primarily the grandchildren to whom I am addressing all these memories, along with faint hopes that a few others might enjoy the story too. I think there has to be a "mirror on the wall" chapter about us all growing up together, I mean Anne and I and our girls Lydia and Jillian. The grandkids might be thrilled to hear about how fractious and exasperating their parents once were. And I am stirred to pass on a few lessons learned, perhaps even some words of advice, whether you care to heed them or not.

There are schools for every conceivable discipline or query you might imagine, from learning how to read cuneiform to understanding the behavior of green frogs in Indonesia who turn yellow for just one day to attract the mating attentions of a female. Surely there is a school somewhere that provides an answer for every possible question you might ask. I am pretty sure though that there is no school anywhere that teaches new parents how to parent, how to be a great parent, when to parent, or even sometimes, why to parent. We are all left adrift on the big sea of life to learn this most important of all human skills all by ourselves. The poor parents are, horror of horrors, even required to use their own beloved children as their laboratory mice while they go to parenting school.

It is not that easy. It is a 24 hour per day job and there are no breaks allowed, nor are you allowed to throw up your hands and walk away. Fortunately, most of us make it through and often the results are quite impressive, although it is nearly impossible to gauge the progress along the way. Slowly but surely they grow up and teach us how to be good parents. Anne and I were no different. We ended up with two loving, talented, and happy daughters. For this miracle I thank our lucky stars and I must also extend special thanks to Anne, Aunt Mary and Chrissie, Grandma Jane, Dave and Lee, John and Ann, Roz and Stu, the Schindlers, the Sherwoods, the MacNiels, the Ryans, and all the other wonderful, caring folks in our little "Village."

When the girls were teenagers we got into several proverbial tests of wills about what decisions they could make independently and what decisions still needed our approval. It seemed that every time they asked for some new independent freedom we would say, "Sorry but the answer is no. You are not old enough. Your mother and I have thought it over and you cannot do that." You can imagine that no's are never well received by teenagers. They would respond with the frustrated rejoinder, "When will we be old enough, then? It's just too convenient for you to say every time that we will one day be able to make that decision ourselves but right now we are too young. That is so unfair! Ohhhh, you two make us so mad."

One night I sat down with them at the kitchen table and drew a graph on one of my classic yellow notepads. The graph was titled "Responsibility." The horizontal axis started on the left at Year Zero and ended on the right at Year 24; it recorded Age. The vertical axis started at zero and rose to 100% at the top; it recorded Responsibility for decisions. Then I drew a data point line from the 100% Responsibility marker at Age Zero, arcing down diagonally across the page to intersect with the Age 18 point, ¾ of the way along the bottom line.

"This graph young ladies is your life. When you are born we can all agree that you have no responsibility for anything in your life, your parents are 100% responsible for everything." Nods all round. I went on, "We also have to acknowledge that at this second point, age 18, in this country you are considered legally responsible for your own life. You can leave home at 18 and make your own way whether we like it or not. We don't necessarily agree with that concept because the age of maturity really should be closer to 24, but 18 is the current law of the land. At 18, we therefore have Zero Responsibility for your decisions, you can make them all if you wish. That's it, girls, simple as pie. Every decision on the inside of this line is ours to make and every decision on the outside of this line is yours to make." That seemed to quell the complaints, at least for a while. The simplicity of this chart was somewhat misleading though because the girls were probably around 14 and 15 at this point, so until they reached 18 there would still be discussions as to whether a specific decision fell below or above the descending line of parental oversight. For example, food choices are pretty safely above the line, clothing choices for teenage daughters are quite often not. Most decisions still required some negotiations, but it helped us all to understand that we were living within a moving matrix and every day the girls were getting more independent. The day would come when they were totally independent;

we would hopefully still have input and share our rationale, but they would be making the final decisions.

Anne and I had both grown up in families that did not have a lot of money; we both applied ourselves intensely at school to make sure we would go on to university and we had to grind through chores and summer jobs to help our families and make enough money for tuition. A scrupulous work ethic was embedded in our psyches. We believe that hard work is the key to achieving what we want in life. Generally, you get out what you put in, whether you are investing in a project, a friendship, or a democracy. The hard work ethic was a common theme in our peer group. Most of our friends who did go on to university created a much more affluent lifestyle for themselves than that of their parents, but they didn't want to spoil their kids by taking necessity and hard work out of their growing up equation. Anne and I took a somewhat different approach. We were very blessed; we managed to make quite a lot of money very early on and we were able to provide many more opportunities and broad horizons for our girls compared to what had been available to us. They were often teased by the gardeners for having "silver spoons" which brought the situation home for us all.

We wanted the girls to travel and see the world as much as possible; there is no better education than first-hand experience and encounters with diverse people and perspectives. We travelled as much as we could as a family and as the girls got closer to that magic age 18 we decided to dispense with the "you should get a summer job at MacDonalds to acquire a work ethic" approach and instead set up an Approved Travel Plan. If the girls focused on their studies, continued to achieve top marks, and went on to university (the more degrees the better), and, if they individually or collec-

The Responsibility Graph—how to lose control gracefully.

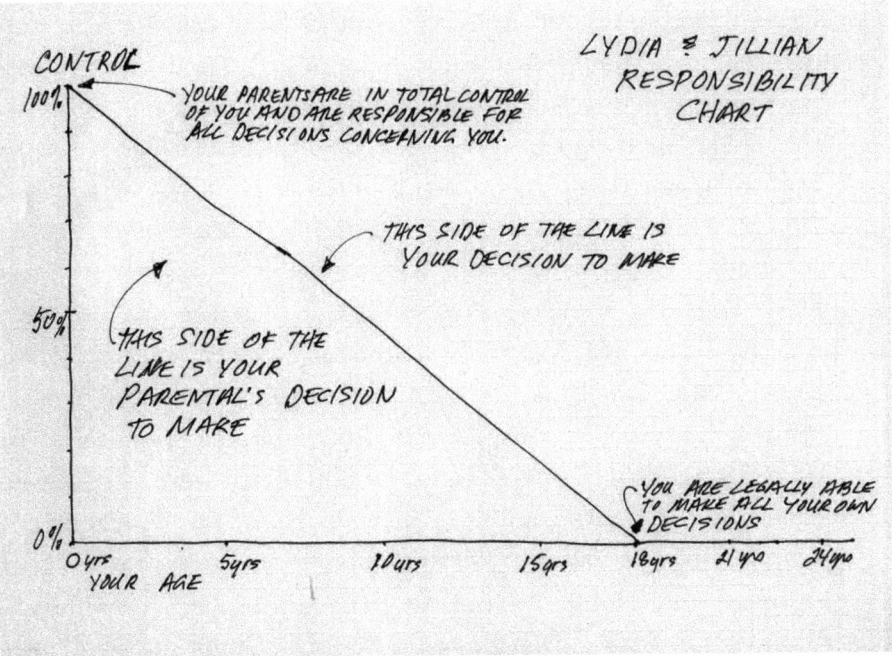

tively presented each spring a summer travel plan that Anne and I agreed was safe and had an educational objective, we would fund their travels, university fees and all of their living expenses. No hammers, just carrots.

Lydia pre-empted the implementation of that program by winning a fantastic $20K Pacific Rim scholarship for study in Asia. She went off after grade 12 graduation for a full year living abroad in Taiwan. The scholarship was designed for young people to gain independence and life experiences by living away from their parents and the BC Provincial government who funded the scholarship actually told us we were not to interrupt this year abroad by visiting our daughter or bringing her home for the holidays. She had an amazing time: she learned to speak Mandarin, taught English, made friends, and gained enough confidence to whip through death defying Taipei traffic on her 150cc motorcycle. At one point she got involved in an expat mud wrestling extravaganza which ended in a lengthy hospital stay for the removal of a two inch spike from her foot, followed by a serious staph infection. She was definitely lonely in the hospital and we should have heeded our instincts to visit her despite the program guidelines. We missed her terribly and we learned an important lesson ourselves: never to let a year's absence get between us and our children ever again. There was a happy ending though because after Lydia's year in Taiwan we all joined her and our little family spent a long lovely summer travelling together as a foursome in China and Thailand.

Jillian decided that with her sister heading off to Taiwan it was time to test out the Approved Travel Plan. Accordingly, she laid out a proposal for a summer in Germany after Grade 11. She was about four months short of 17 years old and we were obviously concerned about her heading off alone, but we wanted the girls to travel as much as they could. The committee approval process was quick and off she flew to Mainz with a EuroRail pass, an envelope stuffed with Deutsch Marks, and plans to meet a friend who had been an exchange student at her high school in Vancouver. Before she left though, there were a few things to discuss. Most parents would give kids a list of "thou shalt nots," viz, no smoking, no drinking, no sex, no drugs, no boyfriends allowed to crash, must call home every week, etc. We did not do that. We figured they were smart kids and basically knew what they wanted to do as young adults and how to behave accordingly. I was very cognizant of the Responsibility Graph and the fact that for Jillian the 18th year was reasonably close.

I said as much to Jillian, adding a morsel of advice that has since become a family aphorism. "You are going off on your own and you are now responsible for yourself, you should explore and have exciting adventures. You will have to make all the important decisions about your friendship group, your behavior, your body, and who you are to become, all by yourself. Only you will be the judge of what is the right or wrong decision for you. Go off and have fun. I ask you to follow only one important rule: Do Not Do Anything Irreversible." And with that she flew the nest.

I know that the advice was effective and memorable because I have heard both girls repeat it to their now adult friends on many occasions. It was an acknowledgement that they were still adolescents, but we were giving them the opportunity and the responsibility to be adults. We knew they would experiment with things, and make some mistakes as we all do, and we know that most experiences are just that, we have all been there, done that. Most difficulties and regrettable experiences are only a temporary phase. Some choices, though, might alter your life forever, might in fact be irreversible—like addiction to hard drugs, getting pregnant, a criminal record, or a facial tattoo. That was a handy measuring stick to consider, then they could come to their own decisions.

Other "bon mots" for independence were not quite so profound but some did become maxims for good behavior. One was passed on to me by my early Kamloops boss in Imperial Oil. We would be out drinking on the first evening of a sales convention or a trade show, everyone would consume way more than they should and at 23 you might expect the next morning would logically be a sleep-in time. Not so. Norm Ross used to say, "Go ahead guys and drink like there will be no tomorrow; you will regret it because there will be a tomorrow and at 8 a.m. the sales meeting starts. You will be in your seat looking bright and cheery or you will be on the bus home. I can't teach you anything about how much you should or should not drink. What I can tell you though, is that the moment your drinking gets in the way of your work responsibilities you have made a choice. We will both have made a choice." It worked for me and I have used those lines or ones adapted for the occasion on many hundreds of employees over my own long career.

Certainly, it was a good rule to have around our own home too. Two pretty teenage daughters, a mother and father who loved to entertain and who just happened to own a brewery, a lovely big cedar party deck overlooking a spacious back yard. Did I mention an endless keg or an icy wheelbarrow full of Granville Island Lager on that back deck? It was all a pretty big draw for their friends in high school and then their friends at university. We welcomed the young people to our house because if they congregated here we knew where everyone was and could keep an eye on the proceedings. We knew all the parental phone numbers and we occasionally would confiscate car keys, call parents, arrange for rides home, or pull out the sleeping bags. Anyone could sleep over and then they would be asked to help with the cleanup and be invited to partake of the fresh crab and croissant brunch at 8 a.m. the next morning. Looking bright and cheery. From my perspective it was all good clean fun, coming of age fun. It was going to happen somewhere, better at our place safely, than somewhere else. What I did insist on for our girls though or for any of their friends living or staying in our house for that matter was that Norm Ross rule. They could have as much beer as they liked as long as they appeared bright eyed and bushy tailed the next morning at breakfast, or the parties were over. Carrots again, though some sticks were displayed nearby.

I have had at least one colossal failure of fatherhood that I have to fess up to. The girls had been away from each other for a long time after travel overseas and one weekend there was a reunion at Marpole. They had such a great time being back home together. We had parties and they went out for lunches and visits and shopping. One day I met them at the door as they came breezing in with arms full of shopping bags. I looked again, shocked. They were both sporting nose rings! I could not believe my eyes. I totally lost it, right then and there. I ranted and raved about how they were defacing themselves and destroying their beauty, how tattoos and piercings were a sign of rebellion. I could not believe they would do that to themselves or to me. One of them said, "Relax dad, it's just jewelry. Stop getting into such a flap." Anne took the girls' side and told me to calm down and that made me even more angry.

I raged on; I even threatened to cut off their support. I said some horrible things. I was a complete madman. Eventually they had had enough. Lydia stood up to me and said, "We don't have to take this crap from you. Come on Jill let's get out of this madhouse, let's go to my apartment. Get your things, we are out of here." Right, she had her own apartment, we were off the graph now. I stormed off to the den; the girls slammed their car doors and drove off; it was all over. Anne came to try to talk sense to me, but I would not listen to anything she had to say. Despite my efforts to distance myself from reason, I registered her saying that her relationship with the girls would continue regardless of what I decided to do.

After a couple of hours of sulking in the den I started to think about what I had done and what they had done, but even then, there seemed to be no way to compromise except if they took those bloody rings out of their noses. Eventually I went down to my office to do some work. There was a handwritten letter on a yellow legal pad sitting on my keyboard. It was in Jillian's distinctive handwriting.

> *Dear Dad, This morning when Lydia and I left the house you kissed us both and told us you loved us. When we came back, you told us that you do not love us anymore. The only thing that changed in that time is one minor aspect of our external appearance, we have acquired these 'ugly' nose rings. That leads us to believe that the only reason you love us is for our looks. I am certain that your love for us is not that shallow. When you come to that realization too, please let us know. Love Jillian*

The simple logic of that straightforward (smartass) statement hit me like a ton of bricks. Instantly my temper tantrum was over. Reality was finally so clear. What a complete and utter idiot I had been. Give your head a shake Mitch. I had set off an avalanche that might engulf our whole family. Why had I let my temper get so out of control? Now I had lost my daughters. Over two silly little nose rings.

My anger had been replaced by fear and remorse, I must attempt to reset the clock. I picked up the phone and dialed Lydia's apartment. She picked up right away. I stammered, "I want to apologize to you Lydia and to Jillian, I can't believe what I have done." She cut in, "It's all right dad. We knew you would come to your senses. We'll be right over!"

They got me. Though in the clarity of retrospect maybe I did win in the end. After four or five years both girls had removed their nose rings. It turns out that decision was reversible!

MAKING WAY : A MEMOIR

TOP LEFT *Little cuties, Lydia and Jillian in the Okanagan in 1979.*

BOTTOM LEFT *Christmas at Norm & Trish Ross's house.*

BELOW *Mitch and Dave Franklin in the middle of a carpentry project.*

LEFT *Family Christmas photo circa 1979.*

BELOW *Our family heading for Maui with the MacNiels: Cameron, Jilly, Mitch, Lydia, Anne, and Tenley in 1984.*

BELOW *We four at a family wedding (Pearl's son Tim Houck) in Calgary AB, circa 1990.*

RIGHT *Incorrigible daughters: one nose stud and one nose ring go sailing in Fiji in 1996.*

A BMI wave attenuator float performing beautifully in New Zealand. Notice the rough waves on the right and calm water on the left.

— 10 —

BELLINGHAM MARINE

One afternoon in late 1993 I was driving over the Lions Gate bridge, returning home after a frustrating afternoon dealing with a house building project in West Vancouver. House building was not going well. My contractor was proving to be unprofessional in many ways. The episode on this particular day had sealed any "good housekeeping award" we might have been hoping for. We were pouring the basement walls; somehow, he had bungled the ready-mix truck order and there was not enough concrete to finish the pour. This was Friday afternoon with no chance of another delivery until Monday morning. That delay would create a cold joint on two of the basement walls about six feet up from the floor which could mean water leaks and possible loss of structural integrity. It also meant I would be selling a less than perfect house probably at a less than perfect price. Remember that this was Vancouver in a 1990s recession, long before the real estate prices went through the roof. My original profit margin budget on a $300K house and property might have been about $100K. We were nowhere near that anymore and still only at the foundation stage.

I clicked on the cd player to sooth my jangled nerves. A Simon and Garfunkel song, "Bridge Over Troubled Waters" brought tears to my eyes as usual:

> *When you're down and out, when you're on the street*
> *When evening falls so hard, I will comfort you*

The Aunt's words rang in my head, "If you can't do something well, Mitch, then don't bother doing it at all." She was right again. This house building business was not my thing and definitely not my passion. In fact, it had been a make work project I had agreed to do after moving on from the sale of Granville Island Brewing. My heart was not into real estate deals or building bloody houses with idiot contractors. It was definitely time to move on.

At this point you might well say, "Hold on here Buddy, last chapter we had just opened the brewery in 1984 and now it is 1993. You can't just fob off a whole decade with no story." OK, point taken.

For a lot of reasons, the brewery project was one of the most exciting ventures I have ever been involved in. There was the excitement of creating something totally new, attracting all those talented young people who just knew it was a winner and wanted to be involved. It was the challenge of blending together all their disparate talents. It was the opportunity to use all my skills to mentor the people and to grow the business from scratch. And pride in the results: seeing a wonderful product being produced to great acclaim, enshrining the genre of craft beer in our city's culture, and receiving the acknowledgement of people we met along the way. On a Sunday morning the lineup for the store opening would stretch around the building. How could someone who helped create all this not be chuffed? That euphoria lasted all through Expo and several years following. I went around and gave speeches, hosted beer tastings and spent a good part of one winter giving entrepreneurial courses on behalf of the Business Development Bank (our federal government).

The flip side of that story was not very euphoric at all. I could not make the brewery financially sustainable at the existing scale. There were two big problems I had not been able to overcome. Problem one was that our volume was constrained by the six week aging cycle of the lager beer. The obvious solution was to expand the storage or aging capacity. That required more capital investment. Initially raising money had been easy because it was such a novel idea. I was somewhat overconfident going in and reasoned that the second and third rounds of fundraising would be just as easy. In reality, raising even the second round was difficult, very difficult, because investors now wanted to see a profitable financial statement before putting in additional capital or they wanted way too much equity to do a deal, in which case the founders might lose control of the quality and original objectives.

The second problem involved distribution costs. We had to do our own distribution, which was fine in the Lower Mainland but very expensive when we wanted to ship to a pub or liquor store on Vancouver Island for example. We solved this issue eventually by contracting with a restaurant food services company for most of our deliveries. But I couldn't solve the first problem to my satisfaction.

For several years I tried everything, from taking the company public on the VSE—the Vancouver Stock Exchange, where I got eaten alive by the sharks and short sellers, costing me a lot of time and personal money to buy back the short sales so the stock price would not be too depressed—to round after round of negotiations with greedy venture capitalists, investment bankers, and merger and acquisition groups ad infinitum. All with little or no success.

Here is a prime example. I was approached by two Aussie businessmen, Alan and David, who purported to own a profitable brewery and winery in Australia. They wanted to invest (I think $1 million as a first tranche) in my now publicly trading company. We had to announce such prospective deals to the stock exchange as soon as possible and then we could do the due diligence and close the agreement months afterwards. Once the deal was announced there was great rejoicing all round and the two Aussies immediately got involved in everything, including optioning a restaurant on Granville Island that would become our pub. One big "if" remained: we had to do due diligence on the assets they were vending into the transaction in exchange for shares of Granville Island Brewing. They had hired SNC Lavalin to provide an engineering report on their Australian brewery and winery and that certified report had been accepted by the VSE as proof of the Aussie's assets and their valuation. We were finally all set up for the future.

Something nagged at me. Why could I not sleep? Yup, I needed to see what was going on for myself. Within a few days I was on a flight to Sydney with Bob Hunt (our GI business consultant, also featured in the Barbados chapter) and 12-year old Jillian (along for the ride). Alan and David toured us around and mounted a charm offensive as our fulltime hosts. The winery in the northeast state of Victoria near the Murray River was operating at low capacity. As we drove on to the property, I was surprised to notice yellow and green blotchy areas in the normally dark green vineyards, which was later revealed to be the dreaded phylloxera. We did not get an honest answer about that until I cornered the winery manager one night after several bottles of wine and port. Jillian was a great help. Not only did we have tons of fun together, but the best part of her being with me was that she had a better sense of character than I did, or at least a radar attuned to the discreditable hairstyles and jewelry preferences of middle-aged men. Neither she, nor Lydia, nor Anne, ever believed in these guys, they thought them flimflammers. How prescient. Of course, I knew better so I kept barging ahead. Jillian was my confidant and my conscience on that trip, and still is for that matter. Back then though, this farmboy forged on until he saw those yellow vines; then we were both on high alert.

Next our group flew on to Brisbane to tour the brewery. There were many diversions for wining, dining, and gambling including a memorable dinner at the casino in Surfers Paradise. After everyone had spent all their money at the gaming tables Alan grandly invited us to a gala dinner at the fanciest casino restaurant. During the "Grandfather port" rounds he boasted that he was such a big name gambler here that the casino manager would soon pop by and comp us the dinner. It never happened, nor had Alan or David managed to keep any money aside to pay for this dinner. Yes, you all know what happened next; Mitch stepped up with his trusty gold Amex card. Alert scale elevated another notch. The next morning with some reluctance they opened the big warehouse doors of the brewery and we saw, piled in a dusty heap in the far corner, a jumble of tanks and pipes that could only with great imagination have been the parts of a brewery in some past or future age. Game over. We went back to Vancouver on the next plane and my fundraising plans were back to square one.

We had discovered Alan and David were untrustworthy, but it was more shocking to me that SNC Lavalin had been so easily corruptible, already in the 1980s, as to agree to a false engineering and valuation report. Now of course we all know that the situation has changed little to our present day, what with their bribery charges from Libya and many other lawsuits in Canada and around the world.

I eventually accepted an offer from International Potters Distilling (who also owned Calona Wines and Pacific Western Brewery) to do a share exchange for Granville Island Brewery. Due to the relative size of the two companies, I went from owning 60% of GIB to only owning 10% of Potters. I also joined the executive team of the much larger company. That was not what I wanted to do for a career. It also meant that I lost control of operations at Granville Island Brewery and could not do anything but look on in dismay as the integrity of the beer declined. Soon our beloved brewmaster had returned to Germany; Potters' union entered and restructured the workplace at GI Brewery; the main production was transferred to Kelowna and the beer began to taste more and more like the big three. Granville Island Brewery did become the most profitable division of International Potters because both the capacity and distribution issues were immediately fixed, but I was not a very happy guy and the same could be said for many of our original partners and employees. Our sparkle had dimmed, and I had lost my passion.

After three years as a VP of Sales and Marketing for Potters, I decided that I needed to be my own boss again. I knew I would be much happier growing a business that I was passionate about and one where I could make a difference. I resigned my position and sold my shares in Potters, which meant I sold my stake in Granville Island Brewing.

And with that yet another era in my life was over.

Now back to "Bridge Over Troubled Waters" and that drive home from West Vancouver in 1993 when I realized it was time for a new venture, something to get excited about and pour my energy into. I was nearly fifty, but I was not ready to spend my days skiing, golfing, reading or building houses. It had to be something that still met all my original conditions of an entrepreneurial challenge and people incubator. So please read on.

Serendipity would favour me. That very weekend I received a call from an old friend who owned Bellingham Marine Industries, the marina engineering company that had built our concrete docks for False Creek Marina in 1973. The gist of that conversation went something like this. Peter was tired and wanted to retire to his yacht and his golf game; his business was equally tired and was losing money; the recession of the early 1990s had hurt them and they had not bounced back. After a nice long chat of friendly socializing, Pete came out with a proposition. "Mitch, we have something wrong here. There you are in Vancouver, retired and frustrated because you cannot find a new venture that gets all your juices flowing. Here I am in Bellingham and all I want to do is to retire because I have no juices left. Why don't we just switch places?" So folks, that is just what we did. Bellingham Marine Industries, Mitch Taylor's floating concrete pathway to world domination—as my girls teased me—soon stretched out before me.

Bellingham Marine had originally been a small ready-mix plant and marine contractor located on several acres of waterfront on C Street in Bellingham Washington. Started by Peter's father in the 1950s, it had been very successful servicing the Pacific Northwest and sending off barge loads of building materials to Alaska. Bellingham is the last US port on the sea route north to Alaska. BMI had developed a lightweight concrete product and obtained a patent for a modular concrete floating dock system, trademarked Unifloat. Each Unifloat module was built around a solid piece of styrofoam and covered with concrete on all six sides. A series of these modules were structurally connected together by heavy wooden waler beams and then anchored to the seafloor with tall piles that allowed the floats to slide up and down with the ocean tides. The buoyant foam core could never sink while the heavy mass of the concrete attenuated waves in the harbour and made the docks incredibly steady to walk on. BMI's product was considered the elite float system in the world; however, their 17-year patent had run its course and there were now several copycat competitors in the marketplace. Pete had expanded to two other divisions, one in Dixon California and another in Jacksonville Florida. They also had licensees in Connecticut, New Zealand, Australia, and Japan. They were losing money, their bank was pressing them, and there was exhaustion amongst the employees. For me it seemed the perfect business turn-around challenge I needed.

I put together an acquisition team of accountants and lawyers and we started our due diligence. I was very worried about the liabilities that would come with buying the shares of the company (Pete's preferred method), especially the environmental liabilities. Some of the plant sites had been operating for many decades, disposing of "who knows what" into the ground and water. In a few months I had collected enough operational and financial data and was ready to make an offer subject to the environmental reports coming back clean. Due to the three manufacturing locations the acquisition would still require several million dollars of investment, including the working capital needed to reinvigorate the company. We would need to get the company's domestic operations profitable again and then start to expand internationally.

Growth was the key word. The original owners were focused on American business and were not thinking globally at all. I saw significant opportunities for international expansion through new products, new plants, mergers and acquisitions. And I had another key "aha" moment during my due diligence period. The company had designers, draftsmen, estimators, and engineers in each of the three plant locations, all operating independently of each other. At times they would be required to work extra long hours to keep up and at other times they had nothing to do.

My realization was that since Al Gore had just invented the internet (tee hee) it was now possible to design and engineer something in Bellingham and transfer those drawings anywhere with a keystroke. If one plant was busy, another less busy location could help them out. Efficiency could improve dramatically. The product could be designed in the USA to our exacting standards but could be built in Australia, Costa Rica or Europe for that matter. It was also possible through the implementation of an ERP (Enterprise Resource Planning system, basically a company-wide interconnected computer software accounting and management system) to control operations anywhere in the world from one office or from one lone laptop computer.

I saw the whole world at our doorstep. BMI already had the best US engineering technology; we would add sophisticated marketing and project management construction capabilities and we would set this sleepy industry on fire. Having been a marina operator for many years I knew exactly what marina owners wanted in a facility to attract and retain the best customers. I could show marina operators how to make serious money running a destination marina (with restaurants, shops, repairs, etc.) rather than think of their business as a boat parking facility. I also saw the first and easiest expansion opportunities to be in Asia, starting with New Zealand, Australia, Hong Kong, Taiwan, Japan, and Thailand, and eventually expanding into China and India. Most of the Asian economies were growing rapidly and there was little competition in the marina development business. Our Japanese licensee was therefore going to be first choice for a financial partner. I was definitely going to need more capital to make all this work.

After lining up all the necessary parts, I cobbled together a subject-to offer and we started into purchase negotiations. That process was made easier because Pete really wanted to sell and he could see that I was a willing and capable buyer. The senior staff at BMI soon cottoned on to the plans and were incredibly positive and supportive. Within a few months we had signed a letter of intent (a heads of agreement) and the lawyers went to work to draw up the purchase and sale agreements while I busied myself with finding some investors. The Japanese were indeed interested and although unbelievably slow in reaching a final decision, they were happy to take a minority position. I (foolishly, as it turned out) also brought in a couple of minority shareholders from Vancouver who had deep pockets and who I reasoned would be very useful to the company if and when we started doing our own destination marina resort development in addition to the marina design-build engineering company.

On January 5th 1995, Pete and I signed the formal Purchase and Sale Agreement in Bellingham and announced the agreement to their senior staff. On the closing date of January 31st everything came together in their lawyer's boardroom in Seattle WA. With two banks of lawyers and assistants facing off across the table, about 10 inches of closing documents were initialed and signed off. I still have the three big cloth-bound books sitting on a dusty shelf in my home office. The very next day I was on the road to the border at 6am to start my big important job as President and CEO of Bellingham Marine Industries.

To describe the next few years as a whirlwind of activity would be an understatement. The tasks involved putting a capable management team together, instilling trust and cooperation in all the staff and getting everyone to buy into a business recovery and stabilization program. Following that would be an aggressive growth cycle, starting by acquiring and installing new software systems (an ERP) to aid and track our progress. Perhaps the most important challenge of all was to empower everyone in the company to step up, be accountable, and work harder. A key element was a plan to incentivize every employee with a profit sharing program so they could benefit from the results of their hard work. We also had, as I always include in every strategic business plan I have ever written, a statement that said, "We must all have fun every day."

The employees of BMI in all three locations did step up, they rallied around and within a few months we were hitting our new objectives. We increased our sales, improved our output, improved our margins, and wonder of wonders, we started to make money. It was an incredible turnaround and it only happened because those wonderful people saw a way to make this work, bought into the vision, and applied themselves vigorously. Within a year or two we were buying out our three licensees in Connecticut, New Zealand, and Australia. We then purchased our main competitor in Australia and soon became the largest marina company in that country. We bought a second plant in Jacksonville to build drystack boat storage buildings. We also moved our small Connecticut operation to a big property in York, Pennsylvania to allow for needed growth in the northeast US.

We now had four robust divisions in the four corners of America (Washington, California, Florida, and Pennsylvania) and another two in New Zealand and Australia. We eventually expanded to plants in Malaysia, Europe, Costa Rica and Dubai. Our revenues went from $12M in 1994 to over $150M in 2006 when I sold the company. At that time, we were manufacturing products in 12 different plants in 8 countries.

What was the key to this success, you ask? Of course, it was the people: smart, hardworking, collaborative, and dedicated people. But it was also a matter of timing. Because we could take advantage of the internet and sophisticated software, we could do things in 1995 that were not possible before. We had laptops that allowed every executive to be anywhere in the world and connect to the ERP system to check the daily KPIs (key performance indicators) and make immediate and informed decisions. We could communicate by cellphone or email to anyone in the company and call up any file or back up data necessary for the job at hand. My very small team of four senior people could roam the world and run that company. We had a staff of engineering, legal, and accounting people situated in the head office in Bellingham, with operating managers and sales people in each regional division where we manufactured the products. We hired as many engineers and MBAs as we could find. We supervised our projects with professional project managers, who were mainly engineers. We made every divisional manager accountable for their own department's performance and we gave them extra financial incentives to meet their budgets. When one plant was under- or over-utilized, we transferred projects to other divisions. We did extensive research and development to keep ahead of the trends, and joined as many international associations as possible to improve our standing in the industry. We were world leaders in marina design, engineering and construction and we worked incredibly hard to earn that recognition. And yes we all had a lot of fun.

Frequent trips between the divisions and to marinas being built in beautiful places made for lots of travel and good times amongst the team members and their families. One trip to Jacksonville included a memorable outing to a Jacksonville Jaguars game. The epic tailgate party was ostensibly just a warmup for the football game, as was the excitement level at the start of the game with a flyover by the USAF fighter jets. The jets flew so low over the stands it shook every bone in the stadium. But that is not the story, which involves beer consumption. The tailgate party was put on by Steve Ryder, our incredible charismatic sales guy for the region, along with his wife Terri and Bobbie Greenman who was one of our key installers. Both of those boys could really drink beer, starting off with maybe a half dozen Buds or more each at the pre-party. Then we took our seats for the hand-over-the-heart national anthem which culminated in the bone jarring Blue Angel flypast.

The game started and more beers started to go down. Every time the vendor came around, I ordered four beers. I soon realized I was out of my league and (along with Terri) started to abstain from drinking every second beer, which Bobbie and Steve generously drank for us to keep the orders consistent at "four beers please." At half time I must have peed for ten minutes and was pretty much done drinking anything but water. Bobbie and Steve were way too busy discussing plays and drinking beer and never even got up during the half time show. I swear that by the time the game ended, triumphantly for the Jaguars, the boys must have consumed 35 beers each. This time they did go to the bathroom thank god. If there was a "biggest bladder in Florida" contest, they would easily have won a shared first prize.

I always invited the directors' spouses to our quarterly board meetings. It was a fun time for them and because we all did so much business travelling this was a chance to share some of those adventures together. We tried to pick a special or strategic destination, maybe we had just finished a signature marina in that port, or we had opened a new division close by. Hawaii was the perennial favourite destination and easily rationalized because it was half-way between Japan and North America. We also included something exciting to do for recreation. Golf was a requirement for the Japanese directors, but I was way more interested in deep sea fishing or visiting historical sites.

One of those trips featured the big island of Hawaii, a fancy beachside resort in Kailua, and a deep sea fishing charter day. The fish boats went out 15 or 20 miles; the waters were quite rough, and the captains told us all to prepare for a long day of possible sea sickness. Anne was diligent as usual, took her Gravol and, as we headed out for a long run offshore she lay down for a wee nap. She fell asleep, we fished for hours, she kept sleeping even when we headed back to port 8 hours later. As we approached the dock Anne finally woke up and sleepily came up on deck to see if she might try her luck in the angling chair. Too bad she didn't get a chance that day because she is a great fisherwoman and often catches the big fish while I go wanting. That day my big fish story was no different, the other four of us on board had not caught so much as a 20 pound mahi mahi let alone that 300 pound yellow fin tuna that I am always so eager to land.

There was a lot of travel involved for the CEO of BMI. For the first six or seven years I clocked more than 300K miles of air travel per year. The frequent flier programs of United Airlines and

Canadian Airlines (and their affiliates) just loved me, as did my girls for supplying them with free airfare for any whim. Here is a random sample taken from my 1998 *Week at a Glance*. (For my young readers that was a physical notebook calendar in which appointments and phone numbers would be inscribed by hand. There was a new version to fill in each year and only one version of it so you had to carry it with you. If you misplaced it or spilled coffee on it you'd be hooped and might miss your airplane.) Monday to Rio de Janeiro, Recife, Brasilia and São Paulo. Thursday to our Norwalk CT office, and to NYC to spend the weekend with Jillian who was then taking her PhD at Columbia University. Home to Vancouver late on Saturday night for a very long sleep because Sunday night Anne and I caught an overnight flight to Sydney, then on to Melbourne, Perth, and back to our BMI headquarters in Brisbane for several more days.

    Anne travelled a lot with me, in fact she retired early from her VSB teaching career to do so. She would catch maybe every third overseas trip, to Australia, or Japan, or London and I know she loved every minute of it. When she was on the road with me I would try to book an extra weekend at the destination so we had more time to explore together. Another plus was that Anne got to know a lot of the people I was dealing with and we became friends with their families. Because I travelled so often, we got bumped up on most flights to business or first class and were often comped fancier suites in swanky hotels.

    Memories flood into my mind. A small plane swooping over the bubbling volcano in Hawaii, dazzling orchid farms in Singapore, sipping a Singapore Sling in the lobby at Raffles Hotel whilst the entire staff lined up across the lobby to welcome some visiting African king who swooped by to the elevators, winery tours and cave exploring in the Margaret River, the beautiful beaches on Langkawi Island, snorkeling on the Great Barrier Reef from Dunk Island, visiting the Himeji Castle with our dear friend Hisashi (a talented carpenter who had worked at False Creek Marinas), the first OMG sight of the Golden Pavilion in Kyoto, this list could go on for pages. Such great memories to cherish forever.

Anne's brother David Franklin came to work with us at our BMI subsidiary, Marine Technologies, in Surfers Paradise south of Brisbane. The plant produced electrical pedestals for marinas, they supplied lighting for the docks and electricity for the boats. The pedestals were designed to be integrated into our Unifloat modules. We also sold them to as many other marinas as we could. Dave and Lee had a few great years living in Australia and provided more reasons for us to visit including one trip that included Anne and David's mother Jane, Uncle George and Aunt Pat. David is on my mind today; we are currently going through a very sad time as our much loved David passed away from cancer this April in Deloraine Manitoba. He was a wonderful big-hearted man and the best possible brother, a truer friend never existed.

When I travelled to a division, I would try to visit a marina construction site, which was not hard because we usually had dozens on the go across the country. On one occasion I decided to drop in on a marina site in the Everglades near Fort Myers Florida. I arrived unannounced in my rental car in the early evening. The BMI construction trailer was unlocked so the boys were close by. I went in and helped myself to a beer. Two beers later the boys returned with the company pickup truck and somewhat sheepishly admitted that they happened to have a freshly shot alligator in the back and they were intending to fix some "gator on the grill" for their dinner. The problem was they had no hunting license and if caught it meant a $5000 fine plus forfeiture of the BMI vehicle. Big dilemma for Mitchie. I bit my tongue and had another beer while partaking of the barbeque, which was pretty tasty, just like chicken (smile). I helped them skid the remains into the water where they were quickly recycled by the gator's brethren. We hosed out the truck bed, I got back into my car and drove to the hotel. I never went to a construction site unannounced again.

What were some hurdles? Well, in the beginning, going out into the bigger world required some cultural adjustments for our team members, including some latent-US-hubris sensitivity training. Folks had to learn that the US was not the be all and end all. For example, other countries — in fact every other country in the world used the metric system, but the USA used imperial. BMI needed to design marinas in Singapore, Panama or Barcelona in metric sizes — not imperial. Believe it or not that inclusion of metric units in our drawings was a very hard "old dog - new tricks" lesson. We also had to learn to convert US dollars to Australian dollars, Spanish pesetas, British pounds or whatever was the local currency. And we had to stop saying, "How much is that in real dollars?" We had to learn to study up on the cultures before we visited.

In Japan for example, you'd have to take a business card in both hands and study it for at least a minute, not just rudely jam it in your shirt pocket. You were expected to happily sing karaoke at night while drinking overpriced and watered down whisky. It was essential to take appropriate gifts to your hosts and receive gifts graciously. And it was very important to learn when a "yes" actually means a "no." In some Asian countries, we became aware that our straight up business style was not the norm; they might value a relationship more than the product so no quick decisions because pressuring them could be considered rude. Moreover, some of our potential customers were not quite so ethical in their business dealings at least from our perspective, so we had to learn to turn down business opportunities when they did not meet our smell test. Mostly here I am talking about "fee" people who would introduce us to deals and then expect a payoff under the table or government agents who would want to buy a marina and add an additional markup to our bid price to pay themselves and their friends. Trust me, that was not the way we did business and the only answer, as First Lady Betty Ford famously instructed, was to "Just say NO."

I can give you a good example of unfamiliar cultural and business styles and how language barriers can complicate things quite a lot. I was having a fairly serious meeting in Sydney with my Japanese partner Masa discussing a marina that we were building in our Brisbane factory for their Japanese customer. We had given them a price in USD to have the completed project loaded into containers on a ship in Brisbane. Masa was not happy and wanted a secret meeting with me. I hired a Japanese/English interpreter for the meeting because neither of us were bilingual. I cannot get into further details here, but the disagreement involved price. I thought he wanted a discount but to my surprise he wanted to increase the price. Our interpreter was from the Canadian Trade Commissioner's office. She said to me (and presumably also to Masa) "Now I am going to tell you what Masa says to you, and then I am going to tell you what he actually means, and do not be surprised, the two statements might differ." It was an eye opening experience and it made me realize why it is so difficult to do business in another culture that you do not properly understand. As strange as it may sound for a businessman who never flinched at selling a wonderful product at a high margin, I refused to increase the price. Masa was furious but never let on in the slightest. I was able to resolve the issue by offering to sell it to my partner's company at my price, and they could resell it to their customer at whatever price they wanted. Masa was happy with that solution. The interpreter's expertise was invaluable, and the fee was money well spent.

One big challenge of a rapidly growing international company was to welcome so many new faces and bring everyone in line with our BMI North American standards while ensuring that every employee in every division was treated equally in every respect. We had to ensure that the employees in other regions and countries felt just as empowered and included as the people headquartered in Bellingham or Florida. We four senior executives were critical to this mission. Serving as company ambassadors, we travelled constantly and extensively to every division and every area of operation. We made big efforts to attend meetings, seminars, dinners and drinks at every conceivable opportunity with our employees. We held quarterly board meetings all over our world, and we included our local employees whenever possible. One annual board meeting was a trip on a cruise ship in the Caribbean for 65 of our managers and their spouses. We chose a cruise with three days of ship time (for meetings) and four days of shore time (for fun). That cruise was a huge morale and team building experience. The staff talked about our adventures together for years afterwards. Another attempt to bridge cultural gaps was a "put yourself in my shoes" exchange program between plants which was happily received but a logistical nightmare to execute. I ended up cleaning trowels and concrete forms in Jacksonville while my exchange plant worker held forth from my chair in Bellingham. We both got an appreciation of what another's workday might look like.

After each year end we would hold a big dinner party in each division and hand out to every employee his or her personal incentive cheque as our acknowledgment of, and gratitude for, their extra effort which helped us exceed our objectives. I would write a personal letter on fancy linen stationery and sign it with my "big deal" ink pen. That inclusive gesture paid dividends over and over again. I recall covertly overhearing a conversation between two hourly paid guys in one of our plants. They were discussing whether they should use up some substandard product in a float they were building in order to meet today's production quota, despite knowing that the problem would probably get caught much later during installation when it would then be someone else's problem. "Don't you dare," said one of them. "You know the QC rules. That will cost BMI more money to fix later, it will come right out of my incentive cheque. Overlooking a mistake is not going to happen while I am working here."

Money became yet another product to manage. We were dealing in so many regions and generally making money on all of our projects, yet in some jurisdictions we paid little or no tax as compared to the US where we paid approximately 33% corporate tax. It was difficult not to sometimes wish we were headquartered in a low tax or tax free jurisdiction. Another wrinkle was that the American IRS was quite aware of the discrepancies in international taxation rates and was therefore über diligent in ensuring that "transfer values" on goods and services exchanged between company divisions were fairly priced and correct and did not unduly favour the entity located in the country with the lowest tax rate. It was frustrating for someone like me who constantly pressed everyone to improve margins to then see those profits get eaten up by high taxes at home. Adding to that growing obsession was the fact that BMI Acquisition Co. (the main US holding company of all these divisions) was majority owned by my holding company in Canada, where in the late 1990s the tax rates were actually 44%. Nor did it help that the big Canadian accounting and legal firms were making fortunes by showing business people like me how to move a company offshore (for example to the Caymans or Barbados) and pay no corporate tax at all. Indeed, several of my entrepreneurial friends were in the process of doing just that already.

So, with the same herd mentality that tricked everyone into investing in the great dot.com bubble at the time, I started to spend considerable time and money researching how we could legally reorganize our company structure so it could be headquartered in a tax free haven. We would still pay sales taxes and all other non-income taxes in each of the jurisdictions, but the final corporate profits would be accumulating tax free offshore. With help from KPMG in London I started to put together a new map for "Mitch Taylor's concrete pathway to tax free world domination." Somewhere along that pathway it began to dawn on me that Mitch Taylor, his wife and his family would also need to be domiciled in that same tax free jurisdiction or else any dividends I might want to take out one day (and trust me we had not yet taken any dividends out so far) would be taxed back in Canada at 44%.

Would my family enjoy living in the BVI, Caymans, or Barbados? I don't think so. Maybe for a short hurrah but not for the long term. What about our relatives, our friends, our girls' academic lives and their careers, our own cultural lives, our involvement in our communities? It just would not work. And then an even bigger ethical question finally surfaced in my parsimonious little brain. What about my personal responsibility as a citizen of a democratic country? Yes, Mitch what about the fact that you have been a lifelong liberal and that you believe governments must play a pivotal role in any country and any just society? You support free health care for all, free education for children, welfare for those who cannot work, a pension for everyone over 65 years old, and yes also federal support programs to resettle refugees and encourage immigration to our great country. A federal government must provide a safety net to help citizens when they need help. It must work to remedy inequality and injustice, and it must make basic services available to all people whether they can afford them or not. Governments can only pay for that by taxing individuals and corporations. How then Mitch do you square the need for your country to collect taxes from its citizens against your latest personal interest in avoiding paying those very same taxes? The only answer was also a quick answer — I could not justify it. I had it all wrong. I needed to stay put and pay my share of taxes and be proud of my contribution to our country's mutualist social fabric and high standard of living. Ours was actually a pretty damn good way of life.

With that realization, I gave my last briefing to my board on the tax free subject and informed them that we were not going to spend any more time on corporate tax planning. We were going to stay headquartered in the USA. Anne and I decided to move from Vancouver to Bellingham to minimize my commute and pay our taxes pursuant to the US/Canada Tax Treaty. My E2 business visa allowed us to live in either country and pay taxes to the country where we lived for more than 183 days per year. Tax free talks were over for good.

Accordingly, in 1998 we bought a beautiful little house on Whatcom Lake in Bellingham, renovated it to our satisfaction, packed up and moved 60 miles south. Even after renovations the Bellingham house had about 3000 square feet whilst our

Vancouver home on Marpole Avenue was twice that size. Fortunately, the Whatcom Lake property also had a four car garage so we were able to use half of the garage to store packing boxes and unused furniture for the eight years we lived there. Our dear daughter Lydia saved our hides by overseeing a holding pattern in Vancouver that enabled us to keep the Marpole Avenue house. She and Juan moved into the lower floor of the house and managed the property by renting out three suites on the third floor.

Living in Bellingham was different than Vancouver to say the least. It was a pretty small town and we no longer had our closest friends nearby nor our season's tickets to the symphony and theatre. Instead we had the lake stretching out from our front lawn and tons of forested trails all around us. Anne and I had a great time being a couple there together. In town there was a decent fish shop, a Trader Joe's, and Henderson's, the most marvelous used book store ever. We couldn't want for more. Our kids, both of them in that sweet spot after finding spouses and before parenting, loved to come and visit (Lydia and Juan every few weeks from Vancouver and Jill and Adam less frequently from New York). They relished the time we had there together, where there was nothing to do but swim, walk, read, cook, chat, and sip gin tonics on the deck or the floating dock.

Life at Bellingham Marine eventually grew more complicated for me. Our aggressive growth plans had put a lot of strain on my relationship with our Japanese partners. They preferred slow growth and even slower board decisions. They wanted to discuss and move cautiously to tackle even the smallest decision. Fortunately, only big decisions got to a board vote, so I was able to manage most issues within my executive team. You can imagine how I, being a "quick brown fox," bridled at anything involving the word slow.

I began to have issues with my two Canadian investors, who were impatient for returns and stirred by a misdirected jealousy that grew in the chasm between their role as directors and my role as both a director and management (President and CEO). They watched as the company grew exponentially, which was beneficial to them of course. But perversely, they didn't enjoy watching my strategies succeed, and seeing how the employees (especially the senior executives and the sales people, who were all making serious amounts of money by then) loved me and my leadership style. They felt left out and unacknowledged. They were happy to take part in lavish board meetings and $10,000 Kobe beef dinners in Tokyo but you could see them bristle, feeling that the senior management deferred to me way too much and did not show enough deference to them. Most importantly they thought that the company's profits should be parcelled out every year in dividends that they would share as shareholders, rather than plowed back into the company for working capital to fuel our exponential growth or for profit-sharing with the employees. They picked up on the "we should slow this ship down" attitude of the Japanese partners and felt that they should receive more respect and way more money. One way would be to align with the Japanese and put Mitch in his place, using a new boardroom coalition to oppose my leadership and management strategies.

In order to run a successful ship, I needed to have a happy crew, but the board meetings were not happy any more. It was time to do something about it. Under pressure from the Japanese I stepped back from the presidency and passed that role on to a very capable senior vice president, Everett Babbitt. This was all happening around the time of the attack on the Twin Towers in New York. In fact, the second plane hit the tower as we were holding a board meeting in Bellingham on September 11th 2001. That day was agonizing for Anne and me because Jill and Adam were living in Brooklyn at the time. Adam worked near the UN building on East 42nd and Jillian commuted through the west side of Manhattan to her classes at Columbia. I adjourned the contentious board meeting and we huddled around our cell phones and the TV for most of the day. I will never forget the sight of a distraught Anne, sporting a double ear infection, the house phone in one hand and her cell phone in the other, perched anxiously on the arm of the sofa in front of the TV. It turned out that both kids were fine although neither could get a cell signal or transportation home for most of the day. Jill hunkered down with some friends on campus and Adam eventually walked home (hitching a ride through the Midtown Tunnel then making his way on foot through Queens to Williamsburg) where I managed to reach him by mid-afternoon. It was a huge relief to find out they were not in any immediate danger.

False Creek Marinas, the holding company of BMIA controlled 51% of the shares; my eventual decision for better or worse was to find someone to buy those shares and for me to move on. An alternative outcome would be that the Japanese partners could offer their shares to me, or this new investor, and depart the business. They had declined to offer their shares to me. I moved away from direct day to day operations and concentrated on finding a buyer for my shares. Only then did I realize that I had been too kind in the early days because I had given the Japanese a first right of refusal should either of us decide to sell our shares. In other words, if someone made a bona fide offer to purchase my shares, and I accepted the offer, the Japanese would have thirty days to decide to buy my shares at that proffered price. And of course, vice versa.

The next few years in my life with Bellingham Marine were not so much fun. I was in limbo, in a state that felt like "my wilderness years" if I can be forgiven another reference to my hero Churchill. Poor WSC had spent at least a decade in his "wilderness years" out of politics before returning to the UK to lead their WWII efforts against Hitler. I spent months and months trying to find an investment banker or a company who wanted to buy 51% of the company but would be resigned to the fact they might have to accept only a "breakup fee" if it so happened that the Japanese decided to exercise their first right of refusal. In that case the potential investor's time and effort would have been wasted. Mostly I spent my time looking for investors on the eastern seaboard, cities like New York, Boston, and Miami. You really have to kiss a lot of frogs as I had already learned during my days trying to find investors for Granville Island Brewing. I can tell you I did my fair share of frog kissing for BMI too. Finally, in 2005 after nearly three years of hard and discouraging efforts and more than $500K of expenses, I found my prince right here in Vancouver. A private investment firm was prepared for the challenge. Over several months we negotiated a deal, which when agreed to and signed was taken to the Japanese to accept or match the price. In typical style they took nearly all of their 30 days to think it over but at the last minute they exercised their right and bought my 51%. Mitch Taylor's floating concrete pathway to world domination was all over.

It was hard to come to grips with the fact that this incredible journey was over so soon, a mere 12 years from start to finish, just when we were making big profits and I might have considered slowing down a little. That said my friends, it would be a mistake to feel sorry for me; I did not feel sorry for myself. The experience with Bellingham Marine was an epic adventure, one of the best working segments of my life. I had built up and cheered on a fantastic team that had accomplished so much in such a short time. I had worked with remarkably talented people all over the world. I had travelled to a great number of beautiful places and we had made great friends along the way. In 2018 when Anne and I were getting our visas for Iran we had to list every country we had ever visited. I loaded an app to help and we ticked off 90 countries, not bad for a couple of farm kids, eh?

I had been a part of a massive undertaking and we had changed the marina development world for the better. BMI was on every major RFP (request for proposal) list in most of the developed waterfront countries. Engineers, developers and owners around the world respected us and trusted us to design and build a superior product. BMI continues with that solid reputation to this day. It is like the confidence you have in purchasing an S Class Mercedes; you just know it is the best and that it will perform flawlessly for a very long time. That makes me feel honoured and delighted.

Better yet, Anne and I had weathered those "wilderness years" in fine fettle. In fact, we had a fantastic time living in Bellingham, having more balance between work and play and just enjoying being together with our little family and friends in a 'cabin' by the lake. But you know, home is where your heart is, and though our hearts were just happy to be anchored together they were also yearning for Vancouver. In 2006, Anne and I moved back to Vancouver, to our lovely old house on Marpole Avenue where we still live today at the time of writing in 2021, some 44 years after we purchased it. We will be forever grateful to Lydia and Juan who helped us out so much by looking after this house and enabling us to keep it. They had fun too though by all reports: after our return, stories soon surfaced and it appeared that we had missed possibly the best party ever held at this residence. Although there have been many parties and despite our personal charms, gregarious friends and exceptional hosting abilities, apparently Lydia and Juan bested all of that. They recounted the story of an ultimate party held by the renters in our absence which included a whole troupe of off-duty circus performers. Who knew? An apple never falls far from its tree.

BMI floats with wooden whalers being loaded onto a truck for delivery.

BELOW *Superyachts tied up to a new fancy BMI marina in southern Florida; our product in use.*

RIGHT *Finished BMI floats with electrical supply pedestals installed.*

LEFT *Dave and Lee Franklin in Australia. Dave managed the Marine Technologies plant in Surfers Paradise that manufactured the pedestals.*

BELOW *Adam Franklin, Mitch and Vicki Franklin, beside massive wave attenuator floats destined for Coal Harbour Marina in Vancouver's inner harbour.*

BELOW *Anne and Mitch on a BMI directors & managers' cruise in the Caribbean.*

TOP RIGHT *Mitch and Anne on a beach, somewhere really nice.*

BOTTOM RIGHT *Our lawn and dock at the house on Whatcom Lake in Bellingham WA.*

An Illegal Apple

The early sun was inching over Mount Baker's bald crown as my beloved 500SEL cruised south along Highway 99 towards my Bellingham office. Sun beams streaking across the sky ignited the few puffs of clouds in the low morning sky. This drive was so easy. I was slouched back in my seat and tapping out the beat to Neil Young's "Rockin' in the Free World" on the steering wheel. The 60 mile commute from my Vancouver home usually took about 70 minutes, including the US border crossing.

As I pulled up to the border there was a lineup in the Speed Pass Lane; that was a bit odd for 6:15 a.m. on a weekday. The vehicle at the guard's kiosk was having a full inspection, all doors open, contents piled out on the roadway, and the poor driver looking very concerned when his face glanced up in the rear view mirror. The officious young border patrol officer was barking orders at a second officer who was now searching the trunk. Full inspections hardly ever happened in the Speed Pass Lane; all users had been pre-approved. Something was amiss here today.

When it was my turn at the kiosk, now already 7 a.m., the officer growled at me as I handed him my Speed Pass. "Turn off your vehicle, put the keys on the dash, take off your sunglasses and hand me your passport. You must remain in your vehicle keeping both hands on the steering wheel." The officer was acting as if I had already done something wrong and I was guilty. I had driven through this border at least four times a week for the past three years, with hardly a word exchanged except a pleasant "good morning." Today was going to be different.

For several minutes the self-important fellow peered at his computer screen, frowning and cross-checking against my passport and US visa which he held in his left hand beside the screen. I protested the delay. I was becoming impatient, my commute was carefully timed for a 7:30 a.m. first meeting at the office and there might still be enough time to arrive just a little late. "You will see from your computer screen that I own a company in Bellingham and that I commute there on a daily basis." The officer scowled down at me. "I don't care what you do on a daily basis. I alone can decide whether to allow you entry into the United States today. I will let you know when I have made that decision."

Whereupon the officer walked around to the passenger side, got into the car and started to examine the contents of the glove box and the console. Uh oh. In the drink holder of my console was the breakfast apple that I had been eating while waiting in the lineup. The officer took out a kleenex, scooped up the apple carefully as if it were explosive, and held it up triumphantly. "Aha! I have caught you. You are attempting to enter the United States with illegal fruit in your possession. Importation of such fruit is specifically prohibited under US Law. You should know better than that."

"Could I just throw the apple into the garbage can over there?" I suggested. "Absolutely not, this is state's evidence. You have committed a crime. I can bar you from entering the US for life if I so choose." This was clearly not the time to argue. The young man was obviously enjoying his unrestrained power. I sat there silently fuming, attempting to look harmless and conciliating. Meanwhile the officer marched back into his kiosk holding his evidence in the tissue and began to type on his computer.

Border patrol officers have the right to make decisions regarding entry without any consultation with superiors and their decisions are unalterable. One can only appeal to the governor of the state. What on earth would I do if I really was banned from entry?

My mind was reeling. Of course, the apple was breakfast, not an attempt at importation or smuggling. It would go into my belly without sullying the habitat or the marketplace of the great USA with foreign seeds or pests. But, the officer didn't want to hear that. In fact, the apple had been imported into Canada from Washington State. Should I try to plead that I was actually eating an American apple? No, he wouldn't want to hear that either. The officer was not looking for reasons to let me in; he was looking for reasons to keep me out. I kept saying to myself, as Anne might if she were in the car, "Please Mitch, just keep quiet. Anything you say now will only make this worse." Remaining quiet was so hard to do when all I could feel was hot, angry self-righteous indignation. I desperately wanted to give this young bugger a piece of my mind. I managed to control myself and said nothing.

The officer eventually came back to the window. "I will allow you entry, but I have entered a citation on your US Visa. You have been apprehended while attempting to import illegal fruit products into the USA. This citation for contraband will remain on your record for your lifetime. Any additional citations will most certainly result in a lifetime ban from our country."

Humbled, shaken, and still seething with anger, I was no longer "Rockin' in the Free World." I eased my car forward under the big banner stretched high across the highway. It read, *Welcome to the USA.*

— 11 —

SEA FEVER

> *I must go down to the seas again, to the lonely sea and the sky,*
> *And all I ask is a tall ship and a star to steer her by;*
> *And the wheel's kick and the wind's song and the white sail's shaking,*
> *And a grey mist on the sea's face, and a grey dawn breaking.*
>
> John Masefield, "Sea Fever"

You cannot have read through this book without pausing to ask yourself, "How does a know-nothing kid who grew up in landlocked Ontario and Manitoba, then pursued a corporate career on dry land, never once mentioning a swim hole, beach party or rowboat, wind up founding a marina business in Vancouver and spending the rest of his life on boats, docks and coasts?" Follow that with, "Come on Mitch, explain yourself, something had to inspire you. What was your Call of the Sea?" Well folks, something did inspire me. As you might have imagined by now, it was a book, well a plethora of books actually. LOL.

Remember that I told you about the provincial mail order lending library in Winnipeg, and my quota of five books to read every month? Well, that was the start. At first I loved westerns, up until say age 12, I couldn't get enough of cowboy stories like Zane Grey's *Riders of the Purple Sage* or *Under the Tonto Rim*. I especially loved plots like *Shane*, where the lone hero rides into town and takes his time shooting all the bad guys, one by one.

As my ranching interests started to wane, I got totally hooked on sea adventures, starting with a book we had in our own library called *Cast Up By The Sea*. I can't remember the full story but it included all the elements of a thriller: hurricanes, shipwrecks, bodies and cargo washed ashore, scavengers on the beach, smugglers, revenue agents, fights, and deaths. Even better than fictional accounts were books about real fighting ships: tales of epic sea battles, brave captains commanding massive man-of-war ships with hundreds of souls on board and three gun decks bristling with cannon, chasing enemies, flaming broadsides, masts and rigging shot away, men screaming from horrible splinter or gunshot wounds, their blood flowing out of the scuppers. At the climax the two huge ships would grind together, point blank broadsides tearing apart the 8 inch thick oak planking, boarding parties fighting their way on to the enemy ship, swords flashing, pistols spouting flames, everywhere clouds of black smoke, the acrid reek of slowmatch, the decks strewn with dead and wounded men. Finally, one side surrenders, the fight is over, the defeated captain presents his sword with military honour to the triumphant captain and becomes his prisoner. Then they go belowdecks and drink several bottles of madeira together. The victor keeps the surrendered ship as his prize of war. Have I got you all excited, yet? Hang on, there's more.

How about a book about a shipwreck survivor who is cast up on the beach after his ship runs aground on a reef, who then has to learn to live off the land, like Robinson Crusoe, on some beautiful palm studded sandy island in the Caribbean while hoping and praying for the sight of a rescue sail on the horizon.

Or one of the salty stories by the master prose stylist Joseph Conrad, who sailed the oceans of the world for twenty years as a merchant seaman during the heyday of the British Empire. He famously narrated the trials of everyday antiheroic seamen and plumbed the depths of their human souls.

How about *Moby Dick*, Herman Melville's masterpiece about captain Ahab on his whaling ship, searching the southern seas to exact revenge on the eponymous giant white sperm whale that bit off his leg on a previous voyage? Or the incredible nonfiction books recounting the voyages of James Cook and George Vancouver as they charted a good deal of the Pacific Ocean from the Antipodes to the west coasts of Canada and Alaska?

By the time I left for university I reckon I had poured through more than a hundred sea stories; it was easy for a young man to dream and imagine being part of some grand adventure. That passionate interest in the sea and sailing ships never left me, in fact it is still pronounced. I have since become an aficionado of the Royal Navy's Age of Sail and can regale you for hours with tales of their incredible feats of exploration, navigation, nautical tactics and political strategy. Our whole family have read and reread the 20 odd volumes of brilliant historical fiction that Patrick O'Brian has written about life aboard a British fighting man of war during the Napoleonic wars, featuring Captain Jack Aubrey and his particular friend (physician, naturalist, and spy) Stephen Maturin. We know every escapade by heart, we can recite lines "as easy as kiss my hand" and thus can make absolute jerks of ourselves in any non-Patrick-O'Brian-leaning-gathering or in the company of real "lubbers."

So back to my story, with apologies for the long digression to help you understand my degree of excitement for this subject. I was therefore a perfect candidate to become a founder of False Creek Marinas in Vancouver in 1973. Our company logo was a three masted barquentine that might have sailed for the East India Company, outfitted with elaborate rigging and banners. My personal entry into the physical act of sailing was somewhat delayed, because it required some spare time as well as access to a vessel. We were incredibly busy, I was working long days, and we had newborn Lydia at home. I did eventually get the opportunity to do some racing at the Royal Vancouver Yacht Club on another member's vessel and I learned a tremendous amount about handling a sailboat. At the end of a race we would warm ourselves with a few rum toddies back at the clubhouse. The truth was that the actual sailing on winter evenings was often brutally cold and I was put off by the tough, nay mean, discipline of a racing captain who must win regardless of the cost to his rigging or the happiness of his crew. I decided my future sailing would be for pleasure and during warm, sunlight hours if at all possible.

We were lucky to make many close friends among our own moorage customers at FCM, which extended our opportunities for both carousing and boating as you might imagine. One gregarious young man, a few years older than us, was a developer fellow called Don Low. He had supervised the building of a Formosa 41-foot sailboat in Taiwan and it had been delivered to FCM for initial outfitting and mast rigging. When Sanuk was ready for its inaugural voyage we gathered round and wished Captain Don and his new crew bon voyage as they set course to Cabo St. Lucas at the tip of the Baha Peninsula in Mexico. The first trip would take about four weeks and cover some 2000 nautical miles. Don had invited Anne and I to fly down to Cabo in February 1975 to help him sail the yacht back to San Diego; this second leg would take two weeks and cover 1000 nautical miles. We were very eager and excited to join the great adventure. We convinced another young marina friend Ben Fraleigh to join us, which was fortuitous because his own stunning 60-foot sailboat, New Horizons, had just been launched and none of the four new owners knew how to sail it. Go figger. Ben was instantly on for that trip.

That left one other item of paramount importance that had to be dealt with. Miss Jillian, four months old and still breastfeeding, and her almost two year old sister, Miss Lydia, had to be left behind. Aunt Mary and her daughter Chris stepped in heroically and offered to look after the girls. Phew, what a decision to weigh, especially for poor Anne, but on the other hand, what an incredible opportunity we did not want to turn down. Anne intrepidly threw in her lot and in early February we jumped on a plane to Cabo. In my assessment Anne turned out to be the most resilient sailor of the group, and her enthusiasm and resilience remain to this day.

The two weeks that followed on board Sanuk had such a wide range of staggering incidents and exploits I think I can best explain the experience by breaking it down into three emotional themes.

Wonder and awe. We woke up in a calm anchorage in the lee of Isla Magdalena, safe from the huge Pacific swells inside the refuge of Magdalena Bay, a protected bay about 150 miles north of Cabo. As we slowly woke up we could hear the intermittent hissing sounds of water and air blowing, combined with low grunts. Anne and I cautiously popped open the hatch above our bunk and were able to kneel on our bed with our heads and shoulders poking out above the deck. The early morning fog was lifting in patches as the hot sun rose over the low mountains to the east. Whale spouts, as far as we could see, countless spouts from thousands of grey whales cavorting about on the surface, totally oblivious to us as every few minutes they exchanged the air in their lungs. They were breathing through their blowholes, just like we do through our noses. It was awesome, fantastical and akin to waking in a dream. We didn't even reach for our cameras; we were utterly spell bound with the beauty of nature. The grey whales used this bay as their winter home, they calved here and replenished their energies for the long migration back into the north Pacific. Whales mating, baby whales glued to their mothers, juveniles cavorting about. Occasionally a huge whale would gambol past, easily as long as our boat and weighing probably twice as much. It was so very humbling to be such an insignificant observer of this incredible scene in a totally undisturbed nature reserve.

Fear, morbid fear, "we-might-not-survive-this" fear. We normally sailed at about six knots (nautical miles per hour), ergo you could not go very far or very fast and you could not outrun the weather. We heard on the SSB radio one morning of a massive weather system bearing down on us from the northwest. We were at least two days sail from any bay of refuge, so we had to hunker down and sail on into the storm. By noon the seas had become confused and the waves were breaking over our bows with every plunge of the yacht into another oncoming crest. The anemometer rose steadily from 15 to 25 to 35 knots and kept climbing as the wind shrieked through the rigging and the wave crests got higher and wilder and white froth streaked past the boat. We had reefed and then double reefed the main and mizzen sails but at 35 knots of wind we decided to get the storm jib down before it was torn away. Ben and I attached lifelines from our bodies to the boat and then crawled forward onto the bowsprit to physically pull down the jib, hank by hank. At this point the boat was pitching and rearing violently with each wave. As the bowsprit would start diving down into the next wave, we had to drop the sail hanks and hang on to the railings with both hands. The sea engulfed us, up to our waists or chests before the plunging boat would shudder and start to surge up again, breaking free of the tons of water pushing down on the decks. As the boat struggled up the next wave, we hurried to take off a few more hanks of the flapping jib before we had to hold on again, eventually stuffing the canvas sail into a bag. Very scary long minutes passed before we were safely back in the cockpit of the yacht.

The storm raged all night, the shrieking wind increasing to well over 40 knots and seas swelling to at least five or six meters. We now had fully reefed sails, the engine running at maximum rpm, and we were not moving through the water. Anne was trying to sleep (euphemistically speaking) tied into her bunk in the aft cabin to keep from being thrown against the ceiling or floor as the boat heaved and tossed about. When the boat crested a sharp wave, the propeller would come clean out of the water with a terrible shudder and then spin or free wheel until it dug back into the next wave. That sound was like the boat grinding onto rocks, and that of course was what she thought was happening. Being below deck was frightening and sleepless for the crew below. It was also terrifying for we three on watch above: strapped into positions around the helm, jaws clenched as the bowsprit dove into an oncoming swell, watching helplessly as the wave climbed up over the for'decks and crashed onto us before gushing off through the scuppers and back into the sea. We held our breath until the yacht started to pull itself up from that watery grave, shuddering free as the crest of each wave passed under us and it all began again.

Euphoria. Anne took the helm as dawn was breaking the next morning and three exhausted boys who hadn't slept all night crashed out below. The peak of the storm had passed leaving in its wake mountainous, widely-spaced rolling waves shaped like undulating hills, maybe a quarter mile apart and hundreds of feet high between crest and trough. At first being at the helm was daunting because it looked as if the boat would drive straight into each oncoming wall of water and disappear, but Sanuk gracefully soared up to each crest, paused for a moment's view of the horizon for miles around before swooshing down into the next trough. Everything seemed to happen in slow motion and was repeated for several more hours. Anne found that as she gained confidence, that sunrise watch turned into one of the most euphoric experiences of her life: a joyous roller coaster ride. I came up on deck later to see full sun, blue sky and a few fluffy clouds drifting slowly across the sky. Dolphins were swimming alongside, crisscrossing our bows and gracefully leaping into the air in unison, playing with us like children. Once again, a time to observe and marvel over our miniscule place in the astonishing natural world around us. When we were able to take a fix on our location at noon, it was determined that we had motored and sailed for 24 hours and had not gained more than a mile or two over the seafloor. Instead of covering some 150 miles in that time period the storm had blown us back an almost equal amount. Thank our stars we had kept the yacht from being blown on to the lee shore which by morning was only a few miles off our starboard bow.

We got to join Don and Ben for many dozens more boating adventures over the years, but memories of that first trip definitely stand out as a seminal experience. After that we were well and truly hooked and boating has played a big part in our lives ever since. In the summers we took our own girls to sail around BC's coastal playgrounds, with Desolation Sound a crowd favourite. In the winters we would often include a special trip to cruise, explore, and snorkel in the British Virgin Islands. For a decade or more we had our own Whitby 41 sailboat, Follow the Sun, stationed in the BVI. We chartered out the boat except for the few weeks each year when we vacationed on her.

Undeterred from our first hurricane ride on Sanuk, we joined Don for some other major boating adventures. Over the next several decades Don was incredibly generous and welcomed us aboard his various yachts as "twofootitis"—an incurable affliction that is common among boaters—compelled him into bigger and better sailboats and then powerboats and eventually to the current motor yacht Endeavour which is some 90 feet long and definitely falls into the "OMG Yacht" category. In 2000, we joined Don for a three month adventure on Endeavour, cruising from San Diego down the Pacific coast, through the Panama Canal, and up along the Atlantic coast to Fort Lauderdale. I wrote about that trip in *Notes From the Wheelhouse*, a mini travelogue that helped whet my appetite for writing. In 2005 we again joined Don for a six week voyage from Fort Lauderdale down through the arc of Caribbean islands to Trinidad; during that trip I also kept a daily travelogue that expanded to include a bit of naval and colonial history. If my enthusiasm for writing is not expended after finishing this memoir I might return to develop more of these accounts into a travel book. As a teaser I'll include a few paragraphs from the daily blog I called *Our Great Ought Five Caribbean Adventure*. Perhaps it will whet your appetite for the sea. I trust that you will not contract twofootitis just by reading about Endeavour.

Day One May 25, 2005
It was 12:25 p.m. when a glistening Awlgrip white Endeavour slipped its mooring lines and slowly glided out into the intercoastal waterway at West Palm Beach Florida, outbound for the Bahamas en route to Trinidad. Our great ought five adventure is underway. The seas are calm, the sky is blue, the outdoor temperature gauge hovers around 100F and all is well with the world. Our company of adventurers includes Captain Don Low and his Lady Wendy, a wonderful nephew Warren Low, new crew members Simon and Veronica, plus Anne and myself. Our course today is towards the lower Bahamian islands of the Greater Exumas some 268 nautical miles to the SSE. Our ETA is noon tomorrow.

Anne and I arrived at the boat late yesterday after attending Adam Lerner's MBA graduation in Austin Texas. Endeavour has been in the shipyard/drydock for several months now receiving major repairs and was launched only this week. Because there was no time for a shakedown cruise, this is it baby. So far we appear to have a few computer glitches with the new navigational system, but we can fall back on the old system which works well even if we have to manually steer the boat along the plotted path. Simon and Veronica are new to the boat as of yesterday and so they too are getting their sea legs aboard Endeavour.

I am sitting in the wheelhouse on an elevated sofa looking forward over the captain's station and the bow. For those of you who have never been aboard such a vessel a description is in order. Named for His Majesty's Sailing Vessel of the same name commanded by famous British naval Captain James Cook, the Endeavour is a Westport motor yacht, a Pacific Northwest styled wheelhouse-with-cockpit vessel of 90 feet. Picture if you will a three story condo on six split levels that is 22 feet wide, 90 feet long, and draws six feet of water.

The lowest level moving aft holds a lavishly decorated owner's stateroom complete with mirrors on the bathroom ceiling and other necessities; a soundproof and waterproof bulkhead; an extremely hot, noisy and smelly engine room that houses the two main 500 horsepower Caterpillar engines and the two diesel electric generators; another serious waterproof bulkhead; the crew quarters which are not functional this trip because they were torn apart with the exhaust system redo; an open cockpit; and then a stout door in the stern leading to the swim grid. The second split level up and forward of the owner's stateroom has three en suite staterooms for guests. Warren is in one, Simon and Veronica in the second, and Anne and I in the third. When Benji joins us in the USVI he may have to sleep on the couch!

The third level up—over the captain's cabin and engine room—is the main public area aboard the yacht; it starts with the galley which is extremely well done up with granite counters and beautiful cherry woodwork, then leads aft to the dining area for eight, and then a spacious deep blue carpeted salon filled with easy chairs and soft leather sofas. Beyond that luxurious main salon, glass doors lead out on to a Lido deck with a built-in outdoor dining/lounge area, and curving stairs each side, leading down to the open cockpit (my fishing spot) and swim grid. Up and forward from the galley is the fourth level wheelhouse or pilothouse, where I currently sit, my favourite place by far. It has all the controls for running the yacht and its myriad systems. In the 1980s, many upgrades and retrofits ago, when the boat was first launched, you would see many dials and switches here, but now the wide dash area is dominated by four computer screens and a radar screen. From the wheelhouse two doors lead out to the side decks, the bow of the boat, and a stairway leading up to the boat deck. The wheelhouse also has a day bed up high where one might take an afternoon nap, and an elevated reclining sofa where one can sit to talk to the helmsman and watch the proceedings in comfort. This is the writer's favourite perch. The boat deck—which is the roof of the salon and an outdoor fifth level—holds the hot tub (no kidding), lounge chairs and sun-tanning area, a wet bar and fridge (again no kidding), the rigid bottom inflatable dingy which is some 20 feet long, the emergency life raft, several lockers and a hydraulic crane for launching said dinghy. Above the pilothouse is the sixth level fly bridge which has another set of controls for running the boat out of doors, complete with a permanent canvas canopy, tables and chairs for the guests to lounge on, and finally a mini gym which consists of a stationary bicycle and a tread-master. We all have come a long way from the days of Sanuk, I might add.

Day Two May 26
I awoke for my watch to see the huge Atlantis hotel towering above the beach on Paradise Island, Bahamas. We had motored all through the night and the morning light found us in the approaches to Nassau. Unfortunately, the schedule does not allow

us to disembark and spend our money in the famous Atlantis Hotel Casino Resort. Our destination today is Warderwick Wells, an Exuma Cays Land and Sea Park. After a wonderful day of cruising through ten-foot deep turquoise waters and a detour through Norman Cay—the home of the bombed out remains of a drug baron's private island replete with a downed DC3 in the shallow waters of the bay—we picked up a mooring buoy at Warderwick Wells in the late afternoon.

This was our first taste of a true Caribbean holiday. We snorkeled in the sparkling and impossibly blue waters, fed some friendly sharks and barracudas right off the swim grid, and hiked along the park trails of the cays in the boiling sunshine. Today has been a three-shirt day so far because of the heat, saltwater, and sweat. Right now, all is calm on Endeavour. I have a Pusser's Rum beside me, and I am writing you from the air conditioned wheelhouse as I look out over a pristine white powder sand ringed bay with half a dozen dazzling white yachts on a string of buoys. Since Pusser's is one of the important minor characters in this tale I should specify that it is "the original Royal Navy rum, made to the Admiralty's specifications" at a venerable old distillery on Tortola BVI.

The smells of dinner waft from the galley. Veronica, our Danish chef, obviously has a lot of talent in that department and I fear for my weight management this trip. After several months of painstakingly trying to lose some weight, successfully I might add, at a pound a week at max, the second centum suddenly looms overnight. Tonight's dinner will be seared marinated steak, roasted carrots and potatoes followed by a meringue and whipped cream dessert in the shape of a swan. Because the anchorage is so calm and the evening a bit cooler the dinner will be served outside on the lido deck without the need for air conditioning. My big important job right now is that I am in charge of choosing the big Barossa reds. One of my privileged duties is to be the chief wine steward on board.

So folks, that is where I got my love of the sea, a romantic's taste for adventure, my own lifelong case of serious Sea Fever. Fortunately for me, Anne caught it too and has been with me on every boating trip we ever made. When not at the helm or strapped to her bunk she can be found invariably on the foredeck with her camera, unless of course she has escaped in a kayak to explore the bay.

PREVIOUS PAGE *Mitchie loves sailing; it's the only way to introduce this set of pictures!*

BELOW *Captain Anne at the helm of Sanuk in 1975.*

RIGHT *Waves climbing aboard Sanuk in the open Pacific; much nastier weather lies ahead.*

BELOW *Mitch fishing with Ben Fraleigh, successfully it would appear.*

TOP RIGHT *A very happy couple sailing in BC.*

BOTTOM RIGHT *Follow the Sun, our Whitby 41 sailboat, at anchor in the British Virgin Islands.*

LEFT *Mitchie in his False Creek Marinas Staff shirt, circa 1985.*

BELOW *Mitch, Nina Sherwood, Carol Schindler, Larry Sherwood and Clive Schindler in the BVI.*

RIGHT *Jillian sailing Follow the Sun.*

BELOW *Mitch and Lydia sailing Follow the Sun.*

BELOW *Don Low's Endeavour visiting the MacNiel's dock on Bowen Island. Anne is on the bow.*

TOP RIGHT *Dan Pratt and Chris Lovato in the Endeavour dinghy in Belize waters in 2000.*

BOTTOM RIGHT *Don and Mitch leaving Vancouver harbour on yet another excellent adventure.*

LEFT *MacNiels sail with us in the Virgin Islands, here at Jost Van Dyck for New Year's Eve: Anne, Cameron, Jocelyn, Lydia, Hugh, Jillian, Tenley in 1990.*

BELOW *Sailing adventures in Fiji, 1996: Lydia, Juan Rostworowski, Jillian, our Fijian skipper Julian, Mitch and Anne.*

BELOW *Anne and Mitch in typical BC coastal weather on Morning Beach, Galiano Island, 2010.*

TOP RIGHT *These four amigos have enjoyed many thousands of miles of seafaring together: Mitch, Anne, Don Low, Ben Fraleigh.*

BOTTOM RIGHT *Anne looking glam.*

BELOW *Martinis made with 10,000 year old glacial ice collected that day in Juneau Alaska, 2006.*

RIGHT *Don, Ben and his son Jake, and Mitch in Alaska.*

TOP LEFT *Looking down from an old British fort overlooking English Harbour in Antigua in 2005.*

BOTTOM LEFT *Anne kayaking in the Broughton Island archipelago BC.*

BELOW *Adam Lerner, Anne, Jillian, Lydia, Juan, and Mitch in Desolation Sound BC, 2000.*

Antiguan Customs & Immigration Explained

While Captain Don took his wife and her friend to the airport, Anne climbed up the hills behind Nelson's Dockyard for some morning photos, and I busied myself clearing our MV Endeavour through Antiguan Customs and Immigration in preparation for an 11 a.m. departure to Guadeloupe.

There would be six of us left aboard Endeavour, a British Island of Guernsey registered private yacht. Our glistening white craft with its three imposing decks and bristling radar and communication masts looked mighty impressive against the historic naval backdrop of Nelson's Dockyard with its two massive stone forts that have guarded the entrance to English Harbour since the 1750s. Indeed, during the time of the famous Admiral Horatio Nelson this Age of Sail harbour had protected many great fleets of Royal Navy warships as they refitted and repaired their double and triple decker battleships in preparation for combat and contests of superiority against the French and Spanish navies.

The Antiguan Customs and Immigration experience is worth a detailed description because, in one form or another, this experience repeats at every Caribbean island. Independent and sovereign nations obviously have the right to decide who comes and goes from their shores and under what protocols, as anyone who visits the incredibly paranoid USA would know. Antigua does it this way.

The tiny stuffy one room office of Customs and Immigration held three ranking officials. I dealt with Level One first as he was standing at the counter when I entered. He watched impassively as I filled in the impossible-to-decipher forms incorrectly and then said, with a superior English accent, "There are no corrections permitted. Here is a new three-part form with two carbons. All five pieces must stay perfectly aligned, or you will have to do it again." I mumbled an apology and started again.

I was on my third attempt at the paperwork when Level Two came over to supervise. Sensing that I was obviously not proficient in the English language he announced authoritatively, "If you carry on that way, sir, we are going to run out of forms. I am going to make an executive decision here and decree that these last few mistakes can be crossed out and corrected, provided they are initialed by both parties." I breathed a sigh of relief.

Antiguan Immigration is not as worried about who visits their island as they are about ensuring that everyone who does visit them leaves as promised. And, perhaps I should have mentioned this first, it must be acknowledged that the Office of Customs and Immigration be held in absolute and complete respect at all times.

I had known enough about the respect part to appear in a freshly pressed white shirt tucked into clean white knee length shorts, and a pair of freshly polished boating shoes.

Unfortunately, we had unwittingly run afoul of the first protocol by bringing in eight people by sea one week ago, and now attempting to leave with only six people aboard, because two of our original eight were leaving the island this morning by airplane.

The possibility that our vessel might leave two people behind on their island elevated me immediately to Level Three, the most senior official in this department. Level Three was a very important and serious fellow. He was dressed in an immaculately pressed and fitted officer's uniform, adorned with badges, chevrons, ribbons and many brass buttons. He wore a crisp white shirt and Windsor knotted black tie. Taking my corrected and initialed manifest, he scanned it severely for several minutes. He then carefully compared the (approved) inbound passenger list to my (as yet unapproved) outbound passenger list.

He looked at me over the counter, incredulously, "You can only leave this island, Mister Taylor, if you take all eight people with you. I see only six passengers and six passports here. Where are the passports of the other two might I ask?" I stammered that our other two guests were this very minute at the airport getting on an Air Canada flight to Toronto.

It appeared to dawn on Level Three that the proof of my statement could only be confirmed by the immigration office at the airport. His face also betrayed a sense that calling the airport might be a very big bother for him.

The three officials repaired to the farthest end of the room away from me. They huddled together and conferred, whispering back and forth with no obvious agreement for several minutes. Then Level Three straightened up and approached the counter. "I have decided that I have the authority to approve this declaration due to the fact that I am actually senior to the immigration officer at the airport. Please declare your manifest true and sign here, I will then approve it, stamp all these forms, and your yacht may leave Antigua."

That was not the end though. Unfortunately, Level One observed that our Captain Don Low had signed us into Antigua and I, only a First Mate, was attempting to sign us out. Level Two spoke up, "I am sorry, but a First Mate is not authorized to sign these forms, it must be the Captain or the ship's Lieutenant." Now what?

I appealed directly to Level Three, "In the British Navy sir, the equivalent of my First Mate position as the first ranking officer under the Captain would be known as Lieutenant. You will also note that I carry a British passport. Would not a British Lieutenant be allowed to sign these forms, sir? I should also point out that MV Endeavour is a British vessel, registered in Guernsey."

Level Three was obviously a student of British naval history and we were indeed meeting in Nelson's Shipyard, named after the great Battle of Trafalgar sea captain, Lord Nelson. He beamed at my logic and declared, "Yes I will accept the signature of a British Lieutenant."

With that the First Mate cum Lieutenant of the MV Endeavour packed up his approved paperwork and marched triumphantly back to the harbour. The shore launch was waiting. Endeavour with its deep throated diesel engines throbbing and its exhaust gases bubbling out under its stern was anxious to steam away on another leg of our Great 2005 Caribbean Adventure.

At 1100 hours, right on schedule, our air horns blasted two long goodbyes, the Antiguan flag, flown as a courtesy to the host country, came fluttering down the masthead and the larger British Ensign reigned again from the stern. MV Endeavour cast off its moorings, slipped out of English Harbour and set a course for the Lesser Antilles. Our destination at a cruising speed of 12 knots was a pristine little anchorage behind Pigeon Island on Guadeloupe in the Lesser Antilles, a five-hour passage to the south.

I had five full hours to change into a fresh shirt and brace myself for the French-speaking-only-please Guadeloupe Customs and Immigration.

One of Knight Signs' signature projects was rebuilding the iconic Orpheum neon sign on Granville Street in Vancouver.

12

NOT THE RETIRING TYPE

> *I've loved, I've laughed and cried*
> *I've had my fill. My share of losing*
> *And now, as tears subside, I find it all*
>   *just so amusing*
>
> Paul Anka, "My Way"

In 2006 when we moved back to Vancouver from Bellingham, I was 62 years old. Was this a good time to retire, do some travelling with Anne and maybe some writing? The answer it seems was certainly not. I am not the retiring type. Soon I was lunching with business brokers and scanning the "investors wanted" columns looking for a new venture. My family was supportive as always, but they were also scratching their heads and wondering why. Lydia said, "Dad, you act like you have money burning a hole in your pocket! You finally have your money out of BMI, what's wrong with putting it in a bank or investing it in real estate or the stock market? Why do you have to invest in another fixer-upper or start-up?" Maybe it was hubris. Do I really think I am smarter than the average Joe? Probably, though the more decisive factor is that a business has people, and I am sustained by the collective enthusiasm, dedication, and imagination of a team of people working with me to make a business thrive. And I still felt there was a lot I could contribute. Owning stocks in the Royal Bank holds no interest for me because it is a passive role, it doesn't offer any strategic or operational challenges or relationships with people who might need or want me. I wanted to buy a business.

I found a small local magazine company that I thought had potential, it was striving to grow into a national company with a digital presence. I bought a large chunk of it and we went to work. It had been founded by a young man who had lots of ideas and energy but had run out of money; it seemed like a perfect opportunity to be both an investor and a mentor. But within months, my dear friends, that promising venture had turned into Nightmare Magazine. I can't begin to tell you all the things that went sideways, but it turned out that the young man had all kinds of issues, and I was not, unfortunately, a psychiatrist. Apparently, he and I had different business ethics and views of reality. At first I couldn't see it, and then I could hardly believe it. I had never been near such a character, but suffice it to say, all the things that I stand for and practice in my business relationships just got me deeper into trouble. Trouble in business nearly always means losing money, which we continued to do. I finally parted ways with him, after my initial investment had been consumed, then I foolishly recharged the bank account and started again. By this time the financial collapse of 2008 had hit the world, and everything started to go into the sewer, including my own Nightmare Magazine. By 2009 I finally woke up, put the company into bankruptcy and wrote off a couple of big $Ms. This was definitely a low point, not only because I felt used by someone I had sustained and encouraged, but also because I was counting on that money for my retirement fund, and the financial crisis had gutted most of my other remaining investments.

During this time I was also working with an investment banker friend, Don Steele, who I have known since university days. His business model was to invest funds from large institutional investors (like pension funds) into small businesses trying to find growth capital or maybe already in financial trouble. He invested on a mezzanine financing basis, i.e. high risk, high interest rates, therefore high returns. His security was always behind the bank's so he would take back the struggling company's shares as additional security. If his injection of money helped the business grow or recover then the owners would pay back the mezzanine financing, repossess their shares, and carry on as before. He had been very successful over a 20 year period but now he wanted to wind down the business. What he had left in the portfolio was five companies that still owed him money. As explained above, until they paid him back, he owned all of their shares. To get Don's loans paid back the businesses had to be either turned around or sold off. That's where I came in. I got involved with four of them and Don kept the fifth, Pacific Bio Energy Corp, which had the biggest investment, to look after himself.

So there I was, as busy as ever. One company was headquartered in Manitoba, and the other three here in the Lower Mainland. All four were losing money, had serious operational problems, and owed large sums of money to the big banks, like BMO, HSBC and RBC, in addition to the sub debt due to Don. I started with the company in Manitoba and within a year or so we had organized a MBO (management buy out) that would work for it and for the very happy employees who got to be shareholders in their own company.

I purchased the second company, a hot tub manufacturer called Pacific Spas, basically for the debt owing to Don. It was already a national company, but we expanded our distribution network and sales coverage into the United Kingdom and Europe. We improved the model range and spa quality with better engineering and reduced manufacturing costs by purchasing components in China. This was in 2007 and 2008 near the beginning of the big transfer to Chinese suppliers. But the world was now starting into a meltdown; the global financial crisis deepened daily, and that tsunami overtook Pacific Spas too. Soon our distributors, especially in the UK and EU, were not paying our receivables and our operating cash reserves started to get squeezed. Our HSBC bank (where Pacific Spas held a working capital loan) had taken some massive write-offs due to excessive subprime holdings and they started to withdraw from commercial banking in Canada. The next thing we heard was that they wanted our operating loan repaid. Squeezed now from both sides we really had little choice. I called everyone together and we went into an orderly shutdown of the business. It was awful to have to disband a commendable team of people. And I had to say goodbye to another bucket of serious hard-earned dollars that should have been earmarked for our retirement. Bugger those fraudulent US subprime mortgage lenders and bugger their greedy bloody banks.

You may say I was irrepressible, or Anne may have just said "stupid" but I soldiered on. After all, there were still two more businesses I had agreed to look after. My new partner Bruno Kristensen moved in to run the third business, Tristar Industries, a big high-tech machining and manufacturing operation that specialized in repairs for pulp and paper mills across North America. We had several problems: the financial crisis had depressed the market so sales were down, the high USD exchange rate was hurting our margins, and we had an intractable union that had made great gains during the salad years leading up to 2008 and were now totally unwilling to give way going forward, regardless of the dire world situation. This was not an opportunity for much charisma and leadership to prevail, it had to be handled with hard-nosed business strategy, often involving meagre choices between greater and lesser evils. Bruno and I worked very hard at turning Tristar around for the next few years but by 2011 we ended up with a strike. We appointed a receiver and eventually sold the complete operation to a giant Austria-based competitor, Andritz, who owns it today. The good news is that the company survived, we managed to salvage all the money due to our creditors and to our friend Don, and we did not lose any personal cash in the transaction. The bad news for Bruno and I was that we definitely did not make any money for ourselves either.

That leaves the fourth and last company on the list, Pacific Sign Group, which did business as Knight Signs. At first, in order to understand the business, I got involved in Knight Signs as the Managing Director of the Board; the day to day operations of the business were being run by a president appointed by our investment banker. Soon, however, I realized that this business was in a lot of trouble although still afloat, and it had great potential. I wanted to get more directly involved in order to manage that potential. Bruno and I negotiated a purchase and sale agreement with Don that let us purchase the company for a reasonable price considering its precarious financial situation in the midst of the greatest economic turndown since the Great Depression. It was my last chance with the four companies to be able to recoup some losses and, with my ever-present optimism, to gain a little back. Because I was thereafter personally involved with Knight Signs for nearly a decade, I am going to spend a little more time explaining what happened there.

One of the most rewarding aspects of owning Knight Signs was, as per usual for me, building relationships with the people involved. But not at first because I generally like to digress a little. In buying Knight Signs we had inherited a group of stressed out people. Some employees had been there from 1996 when Pacific Sign and Design had started up, having broken away from an existing company and taken a core group of people with them to enter into direct competition with their old company. That obviously created a fractious breakup including lawsuits and all kinds of lingering rancor. The main founder of Pacific Signs had been a successful sales guy who fancied himself also a great businessman. He was not, of course, and the company floundered very quickly, not on lack of sales but on profitability. No one at the helm knew how to operate a business. The owner rationalized very quickly that he could make easier money for himself right off the top, by paying himself a percentage of the gross sales he brokered, then—as the self-styled sales manager—taking a percentage of all sales coming in from the other salesmen. So, he did very well for himself, but for the company it was a sure recipe for trouble. If a company cannot make a steady profit eventually it fails, and so did Pacific Signs.

Investment banker Don stepped up and loaned them some money, which they ran through very quickly, then loaned them some more money to buy a competitor in Victoria, Knight Signs.

Yes, that money ran out quickly too. They suffered a financial default, and the investment bankers ended up owning the company shares for all the debt. The usual story. Bruno, one of the investors and my eventual partner in this business, soon unearthed the financial irregularities, so the old owner was thrown out with the wash and a new president was brought in.

I took over as the CEO in 2009 when they still had not turned things around. The Knight Signs people had not merged well with the Pacific Signs people and now there were two culture problems, not just one. It was not a happy workplace. By now the employees did not really trust any kind of owner to be truly interested in their personal successes. A big problem for me because one key part of my leadership has always been trust, accountability, incentives and sharing of the spoils; these all scored low at Knight Signs in 2009. Apart from the operational losses and the impossible defaulted banking situation, there were numerous human issues to deal with. Many of the employees were bitter, underperforming, unappreciated, and unfortunately, like their former owner, a lot of them should never have been working there in the first place. Unlike the employees at BMI, they felt they had been hard done by and were not prepared to dig any deeper for yet another turnaround "expert."

As is my style, I went "all in," got to know how everything worked, and got to know how everyone worked. I made a list of who would and could help resuscitate this company and who would not or could not. The latter group had to go over a period of time. I managed the company as both President and CEO and as soon as Bruno had dealt with Tristar in 2011 he came over as our Chief Financial Officer. Over the next six years, sitting across the room from each other in our big corner office, Bruno became a wonderful friend and of course he was an excellent partner. I can say with some pride and fondness, in a long retrospective view Bruno was the best business partner I have ever had.

We solved the trust problem by just being trustworthy. We slowly solved the "special loans" bank problem by giving the bank every extra cent we made over expenses, and we managed to pay off that crippling debt in three years. Like at BMI, we began to pay sales commissions on a percentage of the estimated gross profit margin, so that each team member would want to improve profits on their selling bids. We instituted a very popular profit-sharing plan for every employee. We held town hall luncheons every month where I would give everyone a "state of the company" update, tell them the truth, answer any type of question, and make a point of acknowledging their collective successes. We soon started to make money from our plant operations as well as our lease portfolio.

All these initiatives helped to improve the confidence of the employees and their respect for the company. Knight Signs benefitted from that positive internal culture, and we began to improve our competence and standing in the marketplace. We bid on ever more challenging projects. One sector that we developed a depth of expertise in was wayfinding and airport signage. Indeed, Knight Signs made virtually every overhead wayfinding sign at YVR with that iconic green paint and outfitted every Translink subway station you walk through in metro Vancouver. We also landed some iconic commissions, like the refurbishing of the 50 foot tall heritage sign at the Orpheum Theatre on Granville Street, and the helicopter installation of new SHAW letters on top of their downtown Vancouver high rise headquarters.

We hired qualified people and treated them well. We soon had 80 plus employees of every nationality you can imagine. One day

Bruno and I decided we would figure out how many countries of birth were represented in our little company, and the answer was 22. We celebrated that diversity at a town hall meeting by adorning our lunchroom walls with a flag fluttering for each country represented in the company. You should have seen their proud faces as the employees filed into the room that day and saw all their cultures celebrated. It made me cry. We followed that up by asking for individual country presentations at each succeeding town hall, the results were heartwarming to behold, and the outcome was that we all learned so much more about each other and the world. Oh yes, and the luncheons often featured the cuisine of the country being showcased, an incredible win and learning experience for us all, especially we UK heritage folks who were brought up on meat and potatoes.

One of the exemplary people we had hired at a job fair was Nazanin Fatemi. Recently moved to Canada from Tehran, she was well educated with both an engineering degree and an MBA. She started in our Estimating Department and became a very good friend. At one of our town halls she gave a brilliant presentation on the culture and history of her native Persia, illustrated with delicious food she brought along. That day was eye opening for a lot of us, especially to underscore the realization that Iran was not a one-dimensional adversary or a bogeyman, regardless of US propaganda at the time. Knowing that Anne and I would love to visit Iran some day, I asked Nazanin about the logistics of travelling to Iran given the present political circumstances. Without a second thought, she answered, "I will take you there myself, I will be your guide, it would be my pleasure." She was incredibly generous and true to her word. A few years later Anne and I took a magnificent trip to Iran, where we were toured and hosted magnanimously by

Nazanin and her family. We ate like royals, had our heads spun by the fascinating history and monuments of the Persian Empire, and learned a great deal about a wonderful country that the US has tried too hard to make into an enemy.

At some point along this happy Knight Signs chapter in my story, I turned 70, and Bruno was only a bit younger. Our morning chats often turned to retirement, and what that might look like, especially what that might look like for our company. We had turned Knight Signs around and it was doing very well, we owed no money, we had gobs of cash in the bank and millions of dollars of contracted work in our backlog, we had a great workforce and the future looked very rosy indeed. When those conditions exist, it is an excellent time to sell your company; you can value the company at a top multiple of your profits and still leave lots of profit on the table for the new owner to realize just by completing the pending backlog. The challenge of any owner/operator retiring is that if there is no one left to operate the business properly it can, and often does, fail soon afterwards. We had that problem covered, because we had Steve Mander, our brilliant Chief Operations Officer, who was already running the day to day operations for us. We promoted Steve to President and made sure he owned some incentive stock in the company along with three other key performing employees. Bruno and I then went out quietly looking for suitors, quietly because we would not want to disrupt the employees or our competitive marketplace. It took two or three years before we found the right match, a competing sign company in Calgary. We negotiated a good price and by May 1, 2017, Bruno and I had closed the transaction and were sitting out on the curb looking wistfully back in through the windows. It had taken me a decade, but I was finally back in the black, our retirement fund now nicely topped up again.

Knowledge Network

It is fitting that I have left this story for the last because the experience was extraordinary and memorable. Ten years serving on the board of directors of Knowledge Network (KN) were as personally rewarding as any undertaking has been in my long career. I was able to employ many of the business and relationship skills that I had honed over many decades of running my own companies for the benefit of a non-profit BC Crown corporation. Most significant for me was that this was not my own venture, I was merely one of a team of experienced people selected by the BC cabinet to reactivate the moribund Open Learning Agency (aka Knowledge Network Corporation) which by 2006 was desperately needing a shot of adrenaline and some sound business strategies to survive. I am pretty sure that Gordon Campbell (the sitting BC Premier at that time) had put my name forward as a director with entrepreneurial business experience to form a counterweight to the other directors whose expertise drew on academic or broadcasting backgrounds. I wondered at the time why I was picked for a public broadcaster like Knowledge Network instead of BC Ferries, BC Hydro, or ICBC but I was a staunch Liberal supporter, and my premier was calling so I went along as a good citizen should when called upon to give back to his community. I didn't wonder for long.

I have to tell you about the first board meeting. We were maybe ten people sitting around the boardroom table at the KN offices in Burnaby. The new chairman asked us to introduce ourselves and describe our backgrounds for the other members. Most of the directors were executives from television broadcasting, university professors, or senior government officials. It was a pretty impressive group of talented people and when it came round to me, I was a little intimidated. I said, "I am just a businessman. I have owned and operated probably 20 different businesses but apart from a brief stint as an almost cable television provider, I know nothing about broadcasting or media. I am not really sure why I was asked to sit on this board, but here I am, and I promise to participate 100%." Snickers all around the table. By the way, this was different. I had sat on a lot of company boards in my career but most times as an owner looking after my own interests. Here I was just a regular director, being asked to advise, govern, and mentor others who would operate the company. Well, I was also a shareholder in KN, as is anyone who lives in British Columbia, and that fact alone was the great equalizer for all directors and was our motivation to work together to make KN successful.

The meeting went on. Everyone had a lot to say on most topics. I did not say much because I truly believe that if you don't have anything important to add you should keep your mouth shut and your ears open. At some point there was a discussion of a broadcast production that required more financial negotiations before we could proceed. The group debated what we should do. I eventually raised my hand timidly and asked to speak. "Is this how you would typically approach this sort of transaction in broadcast circles?" I asked. The answer came back very quickly from the chairman, "Yes of course it is, why would you ask?" With emphasis on the "you." I responded, "Well if you did that in a normal business agreement, you would probably end up going broke." He came back immediately, "Well then, how would you suggest we do it Mr. Taylor?" I laid it all out for them, everyone agreed and away we went. I was in like Flynn.

That first meeting also included an 'in camera' discussion of the current CEO, articulating our priorities to give him new directions. When it was my turn, I shocked them again by saying what to me at least was painfully obvious. "The first thing we have to do is fire this CEO and start a search for a new one. We are never going to revitalize Knowledge Network without a new dynamic leader, full stop." That statement led to setting up a Strategic Planning Committee of three: Ninna Baird, Beth Haddon, and myself. Both women were incredibly intelligent and knew their craft. I had tremendous respect for them and soon the three of us were great friends as well. Ninna knew everything there was to know about the background of KN and its historical/political relationship to the BC government. Beth having been the head of English Broadcasting for the CBC, knew everything there was to know about broadcasting in Canada. I knew a little about putting together strategic plans and running a business, so we set to work.

The first crucial move was installing that new CEO: we needed someone with vision, who was creative and entrepreneurial as opposed to bureaucratic and would be excited about the chance to reset the wheels of Knowledge Network from day one. Beth knew just the man, Rudy Buttignol, who was living in Toronto. Rudy was the exact fresh air we needed. When we approached him, he immediately sat down and wrote his own strategic plan (I think while sitting on a beach in Goa, India), it was what we had hoped to see, the board endorsed it, the BC government bought into it and the rest is history. The revival and subsequent success of KN owes a tremendous amount to Rudy who is still the CEO and will be for many years to come.

Knowledge Network is a rare species in the mediasphere: it is our trusted BC Public Broadcaster. A 100% commercial free television broadcaster and digital streaming service, Knowledge Network accepts no advertising and therefore no advertiser tells it what to do. It exists only to serve the people of BC with programming that is educational, inspiring, artistic, and nourishing of local talent. How refreshing is that statement? The highly rated Knowledge Kids airs during the day and in the evenings adult programming covers a wide range of topics including history, arts, music, culture, health, science, politics, and economics. Highlights include many British detective series, and acclaimed dramas and documentaries such as Emergency Room, Paramedics, and North Shore Search and Rescue, which are all first-rate original series commissioned by KN from BC independent film makers.

Numbers often tell the story. 1.5M viewers in British Columbia now tune into Knowledge Network each week. Knowledge is an incredible success story and an example of public sector initiative and leadership touted around the world within our industry and especially by public broadcasters (like PBS and BBC). All of that on a paltry annual budget of about $13M; half comes from a government grant and the rest from 40,000 plus viewer donations and from various entrepreneurial endeavours. FYI that is under $3 for every person in BC. For perspective, CBC Radio, which is one of the lowest funded public broadcasters in the world, costs $34 per citizen to operate. Currently there is a Knowledge Network Foundation being set up to help secure its future operations. I am immensely proud of this little engine that can, and every citizen of BC should be too.

As I write this memoir Canada (along with the rest of the world) is reeling from many long months of social restrictions and quarantine measures imposed by outbreaks of covid 19. The pandemic has kept so many of us at home and clearly people watch television more when they are stuck at home. As their daily lives have become more isolated and virtual, audiences have gained a greater awareness of the value of local community, trustworthy sources of information, and well-governed public resources. Knowledge belongs to the civic institutions that foster all of these beneficial communal reserves. This vital role is reflected in the fact that for most of this past year, Knowledge Network has expanded its viewership to become the most watched channel in BC in prime time.

Kudos to Rudy and to Knowledge Network.

TOP LEFT *Mitch standing beside the main Knight Signs plant in Delta BC.*

BOTTOM LEFT *Rudy Buttignol, Knowledge Network's CEO, and Mitch share a fun outing together.*

BELOW *Anne and Mitch all dolled up for Nilo and Warren Low's wedding in Palm Springs CA.*

A family crab feast on our back deck to celebrate Anne and Mitch's anniversary.

CONCLUSION

I have drawn inspiration from a song written by a fellow Ontario boy, Paul Anka. I should come clean and ask Mr. Anka if I can borrow some of his wonderful lyrics in my memoir. Being a good salesman, I will use the assumptive close approach, confident that he will surely agree, and come to see things my way. The resonance of this theme should be pretty clear to anyone who has had enough stamina to read all the way through this book. You will have noted Anka's lyrics already in several places and here are a few more lines to help me with the conclusion.

> *To think I did all that*
> *And may I say, not in a shy way*
> *Oh, no, oh, no, not me, I did it my way*

Having traced these tales over seventy-six years, I now have the benefit of a retrospective view, and the challenge of putting my own story in context. Surely there is much more I could impart by reflecting on the massive changes that transformed the world as I grew up in the decades following World War II. A bigger world picture needs to be painted around my own humble journey.

My story could be understood as a typical immigrant's tale, though one shaped by favourable conditions. Modern Canada was defined and amalgamated primarily by immigrants. Here I should pause to acknowledge and lament the atrocious dispossession of First Nations peoples who inhabited these territories long before our arrival and were much more responsible caretakers of its ecosystems. European migration began with the French fur traders who came in the early 1600s and English colonizers who won over the country in 1763. The new nation of Canada invited settlers on a grand scale and from Confederation in 1867 to today it has welcomed over 20 million people to its shores. Indeed, the current Liberal government has a goal of bringing an additional one million new immigrants to Canada over the next three years, which I see as an enlightened approach in this horrible era of increasing protectionism, xenophobia, nationalism, and self-centered populism now sweeping across the globe. We will need to make reconciliation and indigenous self-governance a priority, while also responding humanely to the crises of displacement and forced migration affecting millions on our overcrowded planet.

Typically, immigrants come here seeking a better life for themselves and their families, opportunities for their children to receive an education and to succeed to the highest possible goals. Many immigrants arrive in Canada with nothing but hope, coming from rich cultural backgrounds, but often from countries that are suffering conflicts or deprivations: war, famine, depression and debt-crises, political oppression, religious and class persecution, or the fallout of colonial despoliation. Many see in Canada a chance to escape generational poverty; they are prepared to sacrifice everything so their children or grandchildren can improve their lot in life. In one way or another Anne and I are both products of that incredible experiment in migration, nation building and social improvement. My own break came when my parents decided to send me away from home to live with the Browns. The rest of that story you already know about.

My life has been remarkably different from my father's. He arrived in Canada as a 7 year old boy with his parents and two siblings in 1912, just before World War I. My grandparents had been tradespeople and servants in Scotland, not farmers, and so they found their way to an industrial town in Ontario rather than settling on the prairies, where farm land was given away for free to European settlers who would fence it off and establish dominion. Canada was almost as poor then as the Scotland my dad left behind. His family struggled here in the new world, the "gamekeeper" and his wife did not get an education, then the "woodpiler" and his "spinster" wife did not get an education either. They basically repeated the old country cycle of menial work, a large family, and endless poverty. They could not see a way to break that chain themselves except that they did see a way clear for some of their children. I was very lucky.

We were able to grow up in the economic boom brought on by the end of World War II. It was an era of unprecedented prosperity, which paid for so many national progressive social programs: a free public education for all children, inexpensive access to public universities (originally for returning soldiers), social programs like family allowance for every child, public healthcare for every citizen, unemployment insurance, an old age pension for every

Canadian, another Canada Pension for everyone who had been employed. All of these now commonplace supports were not available to any generation that preceded us. My generation took full advantage of all of that and we were able to quickly make very comfortable lives for ourselves, improve culturally, expand our learning, travel to see the world, and accumulate wealth like our parents could not imagine. Enterprising people could take bigger and bigger risks knowing that a slip up did not mean the poor house or the sponging house, it just meant a reboot. Anne and I were able to leap up into the middle class very quickly after university.

I also fully acknowledge the fact that I was privileged to be a white male of UK heritage (as well as heterosexual and an atheist of an acceptably vague Protestant type). Maturing in Canada in the 1960s I did not experience a class system, exclusion, or discrimination of any kind. I had the very best opportunities for university and employment after graduation. Due to the incredible growth in the economy in the 1960s we also had our pick of jobs. The campuses were thick with recruiters and we never doubted we could land a corporate job in a big city just by sending in a few applications. These were not temporary gigs but reliable ongoing occupations and relationships; it was not unusual for people to be hired straight out of an undergraduate program and remain employed with the same company or bank for their entire careers.

Of course, it is not as if our lives were "bowls of cherries." We ground hard every day to achieve our goals and contribute to our community. But I recognize that we benefited from favourable social conditions, and not everyone in our era had the same opportunities, freedoms, perspectives, and sources of encouragement. As Winston Churchill might have said, "Some bowl, some cherries." I am not a social scientist so I really couldn't say to what extent our trajectory was typical or exceptional, and how much it was shaped by individual choices or external conditions.

I suppose what I'd like to tell my wonderful grandchildren, is that in my experience there was opportunity to be grasped by anyone who was bright, determined, hard-working, resourceful, and a wee bit lucky, and I believe it is still there for you today. You four are very fortunate to all be incredibly intelligent, to have doting parents and grandparents, to have enough financial support to get limitless education and all it now takes is to have the imagination, the will to succeed, and the determination to persevere until you do. Although that formula could not work for my father, it did work for me and it can work for you too. One of the challenges may be that the definition of success will be different for your generation. We had clear goals to jump from the world of rural work and wage labour into a cosmopolitan middle class. You may have to come up with another definition of the good life, and your own strategies for navigating the landscape of purpose, creativity, and responsibility.

Let me impart to you a few insights I can harvest from the perspective of my seven decades. One insight concerns money. One of the wounds from my early life was the grinding poverty that surrounded our family in Ontario, where we lived without indoor plumbing or fresh vegetables in the winter. Even at the Browns we were basically only subsistence farmers although we were healthy and well fed and I did get an education that allowed me to break that mold. It stands to reason then that I started my own career driven to make a lot of money, and I did. Over the ensuing fifty years, it seems that I made and lost money in almost equal proportions. Fortunately, our family's standard of living kept increasing throughout it all, and there was always more winning than losing which resulted in the nice black ledger at the end of the road. But you should know that one of the major lessons I learned on that journey, and quite early on, is that money is not a big deal. Its main purpose is to secure the basic conditions of life so that your time and energy can be freed up and invested in other things: projects that are infused with purpose and imagination; a rich social life; a sense of community, mutual aid, and investment in the care of others; room for intellectual curiosity and wide-ranging thoughts.

After you have enough money to live your chosen lifestyle, true success and happiness are to be found in balancing all those other pursuits and sharing them with those around you. As all the books and movies tell us, the love of your family, friends, and neighbours really does count the most. Love is the one thing you can count on and draw strength and purpose from, no matter how bleak or calamitous the circumstances. I have also found that creating family is a special talent and its own reward. Take it from a foster child, family is something you actively create whether the bonds are genetic or not. I think that's why I found so much joy and meaning in being an entrepreneur. I loved waking up every day to a new set of challenges and out-of-the-box opportunities and having a hand in shaping a communal undertaking and sometimes a local landscape too. And above all, I relished the excitement of working with groups of hopeful, capable people: learning from them, fostering their aspirations, sharing the proceeds, and mentoring young people who want to launch their own businesses.

Another insight concerns our total ignorance regarding the natural environment and our place within it. In fact, for my first five decades our entire society suffered from an appalling neglect and complacency regarding the environment. In our ruthless quest for wealth, growth and efficiency, our industries dug up, pumped out, harvested and cut down most of the living world, with no respect for its biodiversity or capacity for regeneration. We developed chemicals that were life-threatening to all living creatures, and in the process we poisoned and scarred the earth. We consumed so many barrels of oil and produced so much carbon dioxide that the atmosphere warmed alarmingly to the point that today the polar icecaps are melting, seawater levels are rising, and warming ocean temperatures are killing reefs and animals alike.

Some of our friends started warning us in the 1970s —most importantly our dear friend Bill Rees, UBC professor and world renowned environmental scientist who developed the "ecological footprint." Bill's voice has been joined by countless other environmentalists; they have been warning governments and all of society for many decades. No one listened, or no one had the courage to act on what they heard. Even now too few are listening and taking action, when the evidence is everywhere we look. Our short-sighted, oil-addicted, wasteful, greedy world is fast bringing its own demise and is surely going the way of the dodo bird.

Mother Earth has a very slim chance of replenishing herself. If we correct our wrongs, change course dramatically, and start the recovery in your lifetimes we still have a chance. A successful effort will take the complete endorsement and commitment of everyone alive. That includes all governments and all peoples. It will take unselfish behaviour and collective action and humans have not demonstrated much facility with either. I truly despair for mankind and for all the interconnected species and ecosystems of the living planet that suffer the consequences of our greed and exploitation. I especially despair that I too was part of that extractive era and consumption society and I didn't really wake up to the truth until I was in my 50s and our daughters were bringing home dire predictions of our futures. It is an appalling admission that must be made and perhaps my generation's greatest failing. It is a terrible legacy we have left you. I am profoundly sorry for it.

How different will life be for your generation? It's hard to guess, but I suspect it will be a lot more complex than ours, with each individual path more visibly interconnected with and affected by vast global forces and imbalances. I also suspect, in the same breath, that you will do a far better job of dealing with those complexities and reciprocities. I have infinite faith in you.

What did I learn in my life that might help you face whatever comes? I learned that optimistic, confident, dogged determination was my single strongest driver for achieving anything. Be resourceful: do your research, make use of what you have at hand, find a way, question the unquestioned ways, create a new way, try multiple ways, and never quit until the prize is in your hand.

I learned that you can never understand enough about a subject; in other words, get a serious education and don't ever consider it complete. Keep studying, listening, asking questions, ruminating, and discussing; test your assumptions and be open to revising them. I learned that I could never read enough books or articles or periodicals no matter how many piled up in our bookcases, because knowledge is power. And yes, you cheeky imps, I know that bookcases are now online.

I learned that no matter how many people let me down, tried to take advantage of me, or did something cruel that hurt me, it is always better to take the high road. Leave anger behind, take off your armour, lead with openness, trust, humility, generosity, and irrepressible optimism.

I learned that the art of living is best described by imagining a book with a front cover and only three pages plus a back cover.

CONCLUSION

You open the book and on page one there is Yesterday (the past). You can learn from yesterday, but you cannot ever change what happened yesterday, it is done and gone forever. You may change a narrative about the past as part of your intentional thought and action for today, but you cannot go back. When you turn the page, Yesterday is gone and it is Today (the present). You live only in today, you can do or say whatever you want today and make any decisions, changes, actions or plans. But you only have today to do that, not yesterday nor tomorrow, only today. When Today is over you turn the page and you have Tomorrow (the future). You can imagine what will happen tomorrow, you can alter any of those future images and scripts because you, only you, can create your future, and yes you can dream, hope, wish, pray and visualize what you want to have happen. But you cannot fix anything until you turn the page back, and it is a new Today. You can never go back and start again, you can only learn from yesterday, live today, and imagine tomorrow. Do not waste time worrying about or begrudging the past, do what you must do today. Create what you can in the present, be grateful for the opportunity to be present and to share that present with all the other inhabitants of the planet, that is all you have. Carpe Diem folks.

 I have few regrets because of that philosophy, however one of my bittersweet regrets would be that my dear Auntie Winnifred Brown did not live long enough to see me past my career at Imperial Oil. She died when we were still living in Toronto. It would have been so rewarding for her, my greatest early supporter, to see me at various times along my entrepreneurial career. Perhaps on the opening day of Granville Island Brewery when I was interviewed on CBC National television, she might have leaned over to one of her lady friends as they sat around the quilting frame sipping tea, and whispered proudly, "You know, that young Mitchell, he is such a smart boy. I just know he will go far."

My happiness bucket is easily filled to overflowing with memories from a long career, but you know for the most part that bottomless vessel is filled by family, including all the special people I belong to by blood and those equally special people I have adopted or been adopted by along the way. A few of these cherished people in my family-by-choice can be seen in the photos included here. Again, my apologies to those I could not include, my editor was really rather stingy in this department. Each item in this last visual trip down memory lane should spare you from reading at least a thousand words.

These days I am most delighted by my four bright-eyed treasured grandchildren, two clever charismatic daughters and a thoughtful son-in-law, who have had my back at every twist and turn and will buoy me up until my last breath. My most constant, vivid happiness of all is generated unfailingly by my wonderful wife Anne to whom I owe everything. Yes everything. Anne has been a sparkling and unstinting companion, supporter, and advisor every step of the way, through the thrills and spills, richer and poorer, in sickness and in health. She has joined me in dreaming and planning this life and dragging out the holystones to scour the decks and do what is necessary on each new Today. She has stood by me no matter how wildly the wind howls through the rigging or across the boardroom table. She has picked up and glued back together more of my pieces than I care to recount. And she has made our surroundings a home no matter where we are. Thank God she is my partner in life. Thank you, Anne, for your imagination and patience in creating this journey with me, and for allowing me to think all along that I did it my way.

CONCLUSION

Our four grandchildren at Whistler in 2010: Sophie, Matias, Taya and Ian.

BELOW *Anne and I enjoying a performance at the fabled Vienna Opera House in 2016.*

TOP RIGHT *Our Marpole Avenue house has been our family home for the past 44 years.*

BOTTOM RIGHT *Our back yard has hosted many wonderful parties over the decades.*

CONCLUSION

TOP LEFT *Anne's family at Mother Jane's house in Deloraine. Backrow: Matthew Corbet, Anne & Mitch, David Franklin, Elizabeth Corbet, John & Ann Manshreck. Middle row: Lee Franklin, Mother Jane, Jonathan Corbet. Front row: Taya, Lydia & Matias, Katherine Manshreck, Lindsay Corbet, Sarah Manshreck, David Manshreck.*

BOTTOM LEFT *Anne's siblings and spouses: Mitch, John, Elizabeth, Anne, David, Ann, Lee.*

BELOW *All nine Taylor siblings at a 1995 reunion we held at Marpole. Oldest to youngest: Tom, Audrey, Pearl, Bob, Mitch, Richard, Florence, Cheryl and Debra.*

BELOW *Four grandkids celebrate Matias' birthday at the Lerners' in 2016: Ian, Taya, Matias, Sophie.*

TOP RIGHT *Four grandkids play on the beach at Jericho in 2019: Taya, Ian, Sophie and Matias.*

BOTTOM RIGHT *Dave and Lee Franklin with son Adam and daughter Vicki.*

CONCLUSION

BELOW *Mitch and Anne on the peak at Whistler with Black Tusk in the background.*

RIGHT *Our Whistler cabin for the past 35 years, seen from the Valley Trail.*

BELOW *My brother Tom and I out for a walk at Whistler.*

TOP RIGHT *Adam, Sophie, Ian and Jillian at Iguazu Falls in Brazil, 2019.*

BOTTOM RIGHT *Matias, Lydia and Taya on a ranch near Ashcroft BC, 2018.*

CONCLUSION

BELOW *Anne and Mitch on a boat trip to the Patagonia glaciers in Argentina.*

CONCLUSION

BELOW *All nine of us in Maui along with five friendly parrots, 2016.*

FOLLOWING PAGE *Taya, Sophie, Ian and Matias on our back deck at Marpole. Where we like them best.*

ACKNOWLEDGEMENTS

I have a lot of special people to thank for their support in getting this long-discussed memoir into print. Or as Mark Twain might have written if he were alive now, "rumours of the imminent arrival of Mitch Taylor's personal memoirs have been greatly exaggerated." In fact, if the covid-19 pandemic had not swept across our country and decimated all group activities, leaving ample time for such individual housebound endeavors as reorganizing cupboards and writing memoirs, I might still be sitting there at the dining room table pontificating about how I really should sit down one day and write up all these stories.

First and highest on my gratitude deserving list, big time, is my editor, my wonderfully clever art historian daughter, Doctor Jillian, without whose enthusiastic support and wordsmithing expertise this story would have been a mumble jumble of garbled run-on sentences. Her love and her devotion to me and to this project bubbles up on nearly every page you will turn. In fact, one day after she had turned back over to me a particularly pleasing piece, I had the insouciant gall to text her back and say, "Thank you for once again editing this section so beautifully that it looks like I might have written it myself." Jillian has patiently assisted my slow progress while looking after her own family, teaching university and still managing somehow to publish her latest academic book *Experimental Self-Portraits in Early French Photography* published by Routledge in November 2020.

I am also indebted to son-in-law Adam for providing me with constant encouragement while he himself was embarking on an inspiring writing challenge that has set a high intellectual standard. His intensively researched and incredibly well-written *Understory* project is a clarion call to our society for urgent climate change activism and our personal involvement.

Heartfelt thanks to my other wonderful daughter Lydia for cheering me on with her typical keenness, affection, and insight. During this scary and bewildering pandemic, she triumphed a career change that included completing her fourth university degree (to be certified as a high school educator) all the while parenting her children, winning a teaching award, and managing a busy consulting business. Thank you for making the time to assist on the final revision of this project, including essential content contributions and photographic selection.

Finally, I again thank Anne for always being patient and supportive, always available as a loving "listen-to-this-one" sounding board, my veritas influencer and our photographic encyclopedia, not only assisting with the detection, retrieval, selection, and reproduction of photographs but also improving the image quality. Without her steadfast intelligent partnership this wee memoir would likely not exist. During its slow gestation Anne managed to publish her own incredibly impressive art tome *Dune Walks in Namibia and South Africa*. As a fun aside, Anne's coffee table book photographic adventure is so substantial and visually impressive that one dear witty friend in Capetown suggested that "all it needed was attachable legs."

My entire family are always so much fun to be with, they really are the very best family one could ever hope to have. I will be forever grateful for their everlasting unconditional love and support.

www.ingramcontent.com/pod-product-compliance
Lightning Source LLC
Chambersburg PA
CBHW052115200426
43209CB00081B/1991/J